WILLS, TRUSTS AND ESTATE PLANNING

PLANNING

Your Final Act of Love

By

RUSS PIKE, J.D., M.B.A

CONTENTS

PREFACE

WHY WILLS, TRUSTS AND ESTATE PLANNING-YOUR FINAL ACT OF LOVE IS BETTER THAN MOST ESTATE PLANNING BOOKS

Thousands of books have been published on estate planning using Wills and Trusts, and how to avoid Probate so why should you read this one? If you are like most people you know planning for incapacity, long term care costs and the transfer of your assets to your family is important, but you have probably never read a book on estate planning. So why should you read this one? Maybe you know someone who was in an accident and is incapacitated, maybe you have read about the high cost of long term care and how it takes all your money you saved for retirement, or maybe you had a friend or relative who passed away without planning and you saw first-hand how chaotic and stressful handling their estate with no plan was on the family. Whatever the situation, you want to provide a final act of love for your family and have your affairs in order in the case of incapacity, long term care, and death.

In *"**Wills, Trusts and Estate Planning Your Final Act of Love**"*, you will learn about some of your options, become aware of some things that could cause conflict or loss of funds for your family, and learn how to avoid paying taxes that can be avoided with proper planning. This book will prepare you to understand enough about estate planning to meet with an attorney and ask the right questions and communicate your goals.

How You Will Benefit

- You will learn the difference between Will planning and Trust planning;

- You will know the 20 most common estate planning mistakes and how to avoid them;

- You will understand what you have to do to protect your digital assets;

- How to use a Power of Attorney; Medical Directive and HIPAA Privacy Waivers for your benefit;

- What special issues result from second marriages;

- Know the difference between options for persons with disabilities;

- Understand your long term care options and how to pay for long term care; and

- Your options for charitable giving.

You Will Learn How to Save Your Family Time, Money and Stress

I have people come to me in my law practice with problems, losses, and family crisis, that either cannot be fixed or will cost them much more to remedy than if they had done their estate planning when it wasn't raining down on them. I have seen families torn apart, over how to divide property on death. Don't be one of them. Buy this book now.

About the Author

Russ Pike is an engaging speaker, author, and passionate estate and elder law attorney. Russ is known for understanding his client's needs, and explaining complex areas of the law in a way that non-lawyers understand. Russ helps his clients by providing strategies and plans that will not only minimize taxes and protect assets, but will also ensure that wealth is transferred to the person intended. Russ works closely with families to minimize the occurrence of those situations you have heard about where family members are at each other's throats over their inheritance.

Drawing on 30+ years of legal experience, Russ has a unique gift for connecting with his audience and ensuring they walk away with actionable strategies to be prepared for the challenges of mental and physical incapacity, the transfer of wealth at death, and dealing with life's changes. Russ has shared his expertise through his three books, ***"Estate Planning for the Not Yet Wealthy", "I Wasn't Ready Yet-Survivor's Guide to Handling a Loved One's Estate"*** and *"**Wills, Trusts and Estate Planning—Your Final Act of Love.**"*

How to Use this Book

You probably have some questions or planning issues that apply to your special situation. Look at the table of contents and identify the chapters that address your specific problem. While the book is a progression of the estate planning process, each chapter is a stand-alone chapter on a particular topic. Estate planning is not the simplest of subjects to understand. I suggest you read one or two chapters at a setting, highlighting important items and writing your questions in the margins. This will provide you with a list of questions and topics to discuss with your attorney when you are ready to create your estate plan.

The purpose of this book is to provide you with the background to talk with a lawyer. By reading this book you will be better informed and help reduce the legal fees to create your estate plan. You might be tempted to take this information and do it yourself. Don't do self-planning with some of the most important issues you will face such as wealth transfer at death, how to handle a potential incapacity, planning for long term care, minimizing taxes, and saving money on Probate. Mistakes in do it yourself planning to save money now, can cost you and your heirs a lot more in the long run.

This book is not for legal advice. It is designed to give an overview of current law. Estate planning and administration is an area of law that changes frequently. Different states have different laws, so when examples are given of how something is handled in one state, it is for illustration only and not to be consider the law for your state. To keep current you can follow my newsletter which provides articles on estate planning, Probate, taxes and elder law. In addition, I post new materials on my website. For new articles visit my blog at www.Pike-Legal.com. To register for my monthly newsletter, send an email to pdxlawyer1@hotmail.com with "***Newsletter***" in the title.

CHAPTER 1

WHY DO YOU NEED AN ESTATE PLAN?

Keep It Simple

As I sit here and write this introduction, an incident occurred recently that answers the question, "***Why do you need an estate plan?***"

Two very successful friends of my son who, because of the nature of their work, maintained an airstrip in the back of their home, often flew to consulting assignments for major corporations. This week, one of them was flying to work when her plane crashed in a nearby town in a heavy fog and she was killed. Suddenly, in the time from when her husband kissed his wife goodbye in the morning, and before his morning coffee break, his life had been turned upside down.

In another sad situation, a friend in her thirties with two

children, suddenly passed away from an aliment unknown until it caused her death.

I often see people who because they failed to plan, are in a complicated and unpleasant situation that could have been prevented by proper early estate planning. For example, everyone should have a Power of Attorney for financial affairs in the event that they become unable to handle their own financial transactions. If a person does not have a Power of Attorney and is faced with dementia, he may not be able to handle financial transactions, but to appoint someone to act as his financial agent, it will be necessary to go to court and at expend a significant amount of money, in order to have a Guardian and/or Conservator appointed. An individual in this situation could have spent a small amount to have a Power of Attorney drafted, but instead now has to file a Petition in Court.

While nothing can bring back a loved one, planning before you become mentally incompetent or die can reduce or eliminate some of the emotional and financial stress on the family you leave behind. It doesn't matter how much you have when you die. Once you die those left behind face a complex and confusing set of circumstances at a time when they are emotionally drained. You can ease their burden by establishing a clear estate plan while you are still able to do so.

An Instruction Manual for Those You Love

Estate planning is like an instruction manual to those who love you if you become disabled or survive you when you die. It's an instruction manual that tells your family how to address your disability; provides for wealth transfer during your life; provides for wealth transfer death, minimizes taxes so you can leave more to your family, relieves your spouse, significant other or other family members of the tough decisions that have to be made if you become mentally incompetent or are in a life threatening situation. It makes sure that in the case of an emergency someone has access to your medical records and most importantly, it minimizes the emotional and financial burden on your family. Estate planning can be accomplished through the many stages of life. Those stages include wealth accumulation, life changes such as marriage, the birth of children, divorce, unexpected disability, children with special needs, retirement planning, wealth preservation and wealth transfer. However, even more important, it gives you a chance to transfer your legacy that leaves to your loved ones your values, wisdom, life experience and family history.

One Size Estate Planning Does Not Fit All

To successfully complete and plan for all life's events, most people will need a qualified team. Usually the team consists of a financial advisor, estate planning attorney and a CPA.

As an estate planning lawyer I spend hours keeping abreast of tax law changes, federal law changes, state law changes, court decisions, revenue rulings, and other planning changes. Similarly, financial planners keep abreast of strategies to deal with a changing economy, new investment vehicles and new regulations. CPAs are continually educating themselves on new tax laws, reporting requirements and compliance issues.

You may be asking yourself, *"Why should I read this book?"* *"Why should I hire a lawyer to prepare some documents?"* The old saying *"you get what you pay for"* is never truer than when you do your estate planning. You are not paying for some documents, you are paying for an estate planning lawyer's knowledge, experience and analysis of your unique situation. Remember, you are planning how to handle all of your assets in case of incapacity or death. Your family is depending on you to do it right. You can buy software that produces some estate planning documents that are probably prepared by an attorney. Maybe the *"one size fits all"* documents are right for you and your heirs, or maybe they will cause a catastrophe for your heirs. You will never know if you did it right, because it will be too late. In the case of your mental incapacity, you could end up unnecessarily spending your life's estate on healthcare or unnecessarily paying taxes at your death that could have gone to your family.

CHAPTER 2

TWENTY OF THE MOST COMMON WEALTH PLANNING MISTAKES THAT CAN AFFECT YOUR LIFE, WEALTH TRANSFER AND FAMILY HARMONY

No matter what your age, gender, health, whether you are married, single, in a civil union or partnered, how much wealth you have accumulated, how many children you have, or whether your estate plan is simple or complex, there are many aspects of an estate plan that can be dangerous to your health and wealth. The following are a twenty of the most common estate planning errors.

Having No Estate Plan at All

Most people postpone preparing their estate plan until they are in their senior years when they realize that if they take no action, the State will establish a plan for you, share that plan with the public through the court system, implement the State's plan by distributing your assets how the State has pre-determined your assets should be disposed regardless of how you might have wanted to leave your possessions. If you fail to plan, you plan to fail. If you fail to plan, you cannot avoid Probate. Probate, often described as that process where after your death, your estate files a lawsuit to resolve claims against you for the benefit of your creditors, is not only costly and time consuming, but it provides a window for the public to look through to see the distribution of your assets. It makes no difference whether you have a small or large estate.

For young parents with a small estate you need an estate plan to make sure who will be the **Guardian** of your children and raise them, provide for a way to manage your estate, pay for your children's education and be responsible for the overall well-being of your children. Just think how your children would be cared for if you and your wife went out to dinner and a show and were killed on the way home by a drunk driver. Until a permanent **Guardian** is appointed by the court, your children could be cared for by the State. Whether you are old or young, single or married, the worst mistake that you could make is having no estate plan at all.

Improper Use of Joint Title on Property

Many people are told that owning everything jointly allows

for transition of the property to the joint owner who has a right of survivorship when the first person dies. However, that transfer may create tax problems and is not available when the second person dies. Often a surviving parent will jointly title their property with their children thinking they have accomplished a substitute for a Will.

However, titling your property jointly with your child is an irrevocable transfer of interest of your property to your child, which you may not be able to change prior to your death. Also, if you title your personal residence jointly with a child, you may lose a part of your capital gain exclusion if you sell the property before your death. In addition, you will subject your property to creditor claims of your child.

Refusing to Recognize and Have an Asset Protection Plan for Creditors of Your Children Who May Obtain Your Inheritance Either Through Divorce or Through Credit Collection Procedures

If you want simplicity, parents can give the property outright to their child. When the child gets divorced, the ex-son-in law is awarded an interest in the gifted property by the court absent specific planning. On the other hand, should your child develop credit problems, creditors may obtain a judgment and collect your inheritance from your child to satisfy that judgment. Both these problems can be minimized through the proper use of estate planning techniques.

Improper Ownership of Life Insurance

Life insurance is beneficial at the time of death. It provides money to pay expenses, taxes and avoid selling illiquid assets such as the family home or residence. However, absent proper planning, the proceeds of a life insurance policy could be significantly reduced by making the IRS or state a tax beneficiary of your life insurance policy.

If the primary beneficiary of your life insurance policy dies, two problems can arise. If life insurance is not arranged properly, while there is no income tax on the life insurance proceeds, there can be an estate tax, or in a state like Oregon, a state death tax on the insurance proceeds that could have been avoided with proper planning. Second, if the life insurance beneficiary designation does not properly name a secondary beneficiary, you will have problems passing the proceeds to children if they are not of legal age.

Failing to Plan for Disability

The chance of becoming disabled or mentally incompetent during a person's lifetime is significant. Absent advance medical care directives, powers of attorney, or establishment of a trust with a pour over will, there will be increased expenses, delays and open Court proceedings concerning the care of the disabled individual. An incompetence proceeding is not a pretty process.

The second related mistake is failing to provide the finances for long term care if necessary. As an individual ages, there often becomes a point in time when they can no longer take care of themselves. To the extent long term care is needed, consideration should be given to long term care insurance, purchased at an early enough age before it is needed, to preserve the assets of the estate.

Not Enough Money at the Time of Death

Not having enough money at the time of death to pay final expenses, death taxes and perhaps pay off a mortgage is a major problem. Even people who have taxable estates and realize there will be a death tax imposed on the assets they transfer to their family, often fail to consider the Oregon state death tax which is "*decoupled*" from the federal estate tax and is imposed at a much lower level than the federal estate tax. Thus, while an estate may be estate tax free at the federal level, the heirs could be in for a shock when they realize that a significant amount is owed for Oregon state death tax.

Choosing the Wrong Executor or Trustee

Whether it is an Executor for a Probate estate or a trustee to manage a trust that you have left for the benefit of your heirs, selecting the wrong Executor or trustee can destroy the benefit of your pre-death planning. You may want to select family members or a surviving spouse as the trustee of a trust or the Executor of your estate. While having a loved one in charge sounds like a good idea, it may not be your best choice. Being an Executor or trustee is a hard job that takes time, skill, patience, management, and the ability to deal with people with conflicting interest. Not only may your loved one not be qualified, but it may create a conflict between your surviving wife and your children over how property is distributed or an estate or trust is managed. The duties of a trustee or Executor are significant and require management and financial skills. Selecting someone who is incapable of managing the estate up to a fiduciary standard can lead to disaster for the estate, hurt feelings, and conflict among your family.

Trying to Do It Yourself

Though there is software on the market that supposedly provides documents for your own estate plan, such software makes the assumption that *"one size fits all,"* that all state laws are the same, and that both estate and tax laws will remain constant. It doesn't matter whether it is a Will kit or Living Trust kit, neither can provide you with the financial or legal knowledge to make the right selections in drafting the "form" will or living trust.

Your estate, even if small by some standards, represents everything to your spouse and your children. Do you really want to use $39.00 software and hope it fits your situation when you die?

Establishing a Revocable Living Trust and Failing to Fund It

It has often been said that knowledge is power. However, what is really power is to take that knowledge and implement it. The same is true with a trust. With the assistance of an attorney, a trust can be set up to meet your specific goals, minimize taxes, and retain your privacy. However, a trust is ineffective until assets are transferred to the trust. Initially, after setting up your trust, assets must be properly transferred to the trust. Further, as assets are exchanged, for example selling one piece of property and acquiring another, the new piece of property must be titled in the name of the trust. Whatever is not titled in the name of the trust will be subject to public Probate and part of your taxable estate.

Not Doing an Estate Plan While a Divorce is Pending

If you get a divorce, your ex-spouse will automatically be disinherited. But what if you die or become disabled before the divorce is final? In that case, your soon-to-be ex-spouse would still inherit under your will or trust. While a court may make specific orders regarding property during the divorce, to the extent possible a soon-to-be divorced person should plan as soon as they are served or serve divorce papers. Not only is who will inherit your property at issue, but should you be in an accident, your soon-to-be ex-spouse may be the one you designated to make medical decisions regarding your treatment, have access to your medical records, and make any "pull the plug" decisions for you. It is very important to change your estate plan as soon as a divorce is filed. Further, once the divorce is final, subject to the terms of your divorce decree, you need not only to change your estate plan, but to change beneficiary designations on employee retirement plans, life insurance, and any other assets that will pass by beneficiary designation.

Mishandling of IRA and Qualified Plan Beneficiary Designations

For estate planning purposes, the designation of beneficiaries on IRA and other qualified plans is critical. When a person has a taxable estate, handling an IRA improperly and not designating beneficiaries correctly can mean that the person who receives your IRA may have to liquidate the IRA and pay taxes within 5 years or less. Properly handled, both income and estate tax can be deferred and the assets in the IRA can continue to grow tax deferred for decades. If properly handled it's possible for a parent's IRA to fund his children's retirement and grow to a very large sum before any withdrawals have to be made from the account.

Poor Record Keeping

Whether your estate planning is done by will or by trust, at the time you become mentally incompetent or die, someone will have to marshal your assets, locate all bank accounts, insurance policies and other assets. Someone will have to determine what liabilities you have and if your debts are secured or unsecured. In addition, an Executor or trustee will have to collect all of your personal property in order to distribute it according to your wishes. It is imperative that you make and continually update a list of where your assets are located, the names and addresses of your closest advisors such as attorney, CPA and financial advisor, copies of previous years' tax returns, bank account numbers, life insurance policy copies and any other record that will aid the Executor or trustee in collecting your assets and making the proper distributions. Make sure that someone else is aware of where this record is kept.

Failure to Review and Update Your Estate Plan

An estate plan is not a one-time event. Your plan changes with your life, changes in the law, changes in taxes and changes in your personal circumstances. Failing to address these changes can result in payment of additional taxes, family disputes, and a distribution plan that was not what you intended. In order to keep your plan current, you should review it each time there is a change in your life circumstances, such as moving to a new state, birth of a child or grandchild, marriage, divorce, death of an intended beneficiary or divorces by beneficiaries. In addition, because of changes in tax, Probate and trust laws, you should have your estate plan reviewed every three to five years. I have looked at plans twenty years old and with all the changes in law and in life's circumstances, they are sorely out dated.

Failure to Create a Business Succession Plan

The majority of businesses in the United States are closely held family owned businesses. The vast majority of family owned business owners want to pass down the business to their children or grandchildren. However, many family owned businesses have no plan in place to pass the business to the second generation. Not only must you have a tax and estate plan in place, but tax considerations have to be part of your business succession plan. If you want to beat the odds and have the family business stay in the family for generations you will have to have a properly drafted business succession plan as well as a properly executed estate plan.

Leaving Money Outright to Minor Children

The most often goal I hear when couples first come in the office to do their estate plan is that they want to keep it simple and leave everything to their spouse. The problem is when the second spouse dies the next step in their plan is to leave everything to their children.

The children may be young or immature, so that if they receive a large sum of money, it may be spent within a very short period of time. Even if all children are twenty-one, they may not be able to handle a large inheritance left directly to them. To address this situation, estate planning documents often provide that the inheritance will be kept in trust and paid out at some predetermined age such as thirty-five. During the period before the children reach thirty-five, they will have access to income and potentially principal for their health, education, support and maintenance. If children are minors when you die, you will have to leave their inheritance to someone to manage for them until they are legally adults.

Missing a Disclaimer Deadline

Most non-lawyers are not aware of what is a qualified disclaimer. A disclaimer is a refusal to accept an inheritance. A disclaimer is often used in estate planning so that a surviving spouse can take a second look at the time of the death of the first spouse and determine whether the situation has changed such that a qualified disclaimer complying with IRS requirements should be made to minimize overall taxes. For example, if everything is left to the surviving spouse, the surviving spouse may want to disclaim half so that it passes directly to the children, perhaps through trust, and the other half passes through a credit shelter trust for the benefit of the surviving spouse. If the disclaimer is properly made, it can reduce the size of the taxable estate and potentially reduce the estate tax. Qualified disclaimers must be made in writing with nine months after the decedent's death. While they are an important planning tool, failure to meet the deadline can result in disastrous effects on taxation of the estate.

Adding Someone to Your Bank Account

Often, when there is a single parent still living, that parent will add a child or someone else to their bank account so that if something happens to them, that person will have access to some immediate cash. The problem is, once you have added someone to your bank account, you are at their mercy as to whether or not they spend your money since you have now given them authority to write checks on the account.

However, having someone take advantage of you is not the only problem you have with joint bank accounts. By having a joint bank account, you have subjected your account to the creditors of the joint account holder and may subject the account to garnishment for any tax lien or unpaid debt of the joint account holder.

When you are elderly you may need help managing your finances. What should be done is to see an attorney and appoint an agent using a durable Power of Attorney, and give them authority to manage your affairs, therefore not exposing your assets to another person's creditors or the taxing authorities. This can also be done through a revocable living trust if your estate is large enough to justify the cost of preparing the trust.

Estate planning is unique to each individual. There is no such thing as a one size fits all estate plan. While proper planning can reduce federal income and estate taxes, and Oregon death taxes, and help avoid conflict among your heirs, even with estate planning there are some common mistakes that occur repeatedly. The above is small list of some of the common mistakes, but there are many other issues that can harm your estate plan. Having a clear estate plan can provide peace of mind and insure that your heirs will get maximum benefit from what you leave to them.

Not Planning for Your Digital Assets

When you die your spouse may not have access to your digital assets. No list of passwords and user names is available. The Executor or your trustee needs to pay bills, determine debts, and maintain finances during Probate, but cannot access your accounts. Automatic payments are deducted from your checking account and the Executor cannot stop the payments. Leave the passwords and user identification in a safe place and let your Executor or trustee know where to find them.

Forgetting Your Pets

If you forget about your pets, when you die your pet may follow you to the grave. Set up a pet trust to care for your pet before you die. Discuss care for your pet with the caregiver and make sure they know how to treat your pet. Provide adequate finances so that care for your pet will not be a burden on the care giver. Make sure the caregiver is willing to accept the responsibility and gets along with your pet.

Understating the Value of Your Life or the Life of Your Spouse

If you have debt, minor children, other dependents, limited assets, or a large mortgage, life insurance can be a life saver. Just imagine your family without your income and with a big mortgage after your death. Value your life and protect your family.

CHAPTER 3

HOW TO AVOID SENDING YOUR CHILDREN AND SPOUSE THROUGH PROBATE

Don't Sue Yourself After Your Death in Probate Court

Probate is the process where your estate sues you at your expense for the benefit of your creditors, so you can transfer your assets after your death. If you have a Will, your heirs will have to file a lawsuit. After the lawsuit is filed, the court will determine ownership of your property, address all debts, claims and taxes, and eventually determine who, including your creditors and the taxing agencies, is entitled to your property and, if anything is left, distribute your assets. The entire proceeding not only is paid for by your estate, but it is open to the public.

The State Has a Plan for You If You Don't Plan

In Oregon, as in most states, unless all your property is held in trust at your death, your estate will have to file this lawsuit. If you have a Will, your assets will go through the lawsuit process. If you do not have a Will and have not done any estate planning, your State has a plan for you. For example, the State of Oregon has what is called the law of intestacy. If you fail to provide for distribution of your assets upon death, the State of Oregon will determine how your assets are distributed. Under Oregon law, if there is no issue of the decedent, all of the net intestate estate goes to the surviving spouse.

Intestacy can create results that you would have never intended if you had planned while you were alive. For example, if you die while you are going through a divorce and you have not done any estate planning, your soon-to-be ex-spouse will typically be able to inherit some or all of your estate. Or, if you have no spouse or children, your assets may go to parents or siblings when you would never have wanted your brother or sister to inherit anything.

Why Would You Want to Avoid Probate?

You must understand that whether you have a living trust, a transfer on death provision, joint accounts, transfer by beneficiary designation, or go through Probate, the resulting death tax will be the same. If you force your children and spouse to go through Probate, you should consider that Probate is a public process. It is a lawsuit filed against yourself that requires court supervision and will require a bond for your Executor. It can be expensive and time consuming, and it may not result in distribution of your assets as you would have desired. Probate gives the world a view of your assets, your debts, personal information and what your family will inherit. Because it is a public process supervised by the court, it will increase likelihood of conflict among your heirs, bring legal challenges, and trigger the solicitation of investment scams and business proposals to your heirs who may fail to have the financial maturity to deal with constant contacts regarding their newfound wealth.

It's Only Money

Probate can be a very expensive process. Estimates vary depending upon each estate as to what the Probate costs can be. While a Living Trust may cost slightly more than preparing a Will, the cost difference is usually small compared to the cost of Probate. In addition, if you have property in more than one state and you do not have a Living Trust, then you will have to open up Probate where you have property. The advantage to avoiding Probate is the delays of the Probate process occurring during the grieving process. Most Probates take about six to eighteen months to complete. The beneficiaries must wait to receive their inheritance until process is completed.

I Want to Sue Myself and Do it in Public Probate

Probate is a lawsuit that you file against yourself, with your own money, for the protection of your heirs and to satisfy the claims of your creditors. The beneficiary of Probate is your creditors. Your creditors have access to court records nationwide and can start the collection process once they learn of your death. Until recently, a major benefit of the probate proceeding was the procedure for handling claims of the dead person's creditors. However, Oregon recently enacted its version of the Uniform Trust Code so that the benefit handling resolving and ending creditor claims is now provided for without the public show of probate. Under the Trust Code there is a time limit on handling creditor claims.

You go through the pain of probate or use a trust with statutory provisions to cover many unexpected situations such as adopted children, second marriages, or divorce. When consulting with your attorney regarding whether you want your estate to go through probate, you should consider that the probate court process means that you are resolving disputes about the distribution of your assets under defined rules. The court will have to approve everything that is done in the administration of the estate. Everything done in the probate court will be of a public nature and there is no confidentiality of the probate process. Do you want to sue yourself with your money from the grave, pay lawyer and Executor fees that will be incurred, have your family suffer during the time delay in distributing your assets, and potentially create emotional conflict among your family?

How Long Will It Take to Sue Myself in Probate?

The length of Probate depends on which state you are in, how many creditors file claims, who will contest the will, what problems occur in gathering assets, how long the process of valuation of assets takes to complete, and many other factors. A simple straightforward Probate in Oregon at the current time with no complications takes about 9-12 months. A goal in my office is to complete a Probate within a year. Some do, some do not. Probate in other states are longer. If you own real estate outside of Oregon you will have to open two Probates, one in Oregon and one in the state where you own real estate.

CHAPTER 4

CONSERVING YOUR ASSETS WITH FOUR BASIC DOCUMENTS

No one wants to think about their own death. For many people, getting a Will is a very unpleasant experience. According to an April 2014 survey by Rocket Lawyer, 64% of people do not have even a Will. Regardless of your situation -- married or single, a parent or no children, middle income, wealthy, a second marriage, with or without grandchildren -- you need a Will, Power of Attorney, Medical Directive and HIPAA Privacy Release. In many situations you may also need a Trust.

The first step to estate planning is building your estate. All through your lifetime, you have developed a financial plan, set goals, and established a program to save and invest to meet those specific goals. Conserving your assets is another aspect of estate planning. Estate planning is designed to minimize taxes, prepare for unexpected expenses that can diminish the value of your estate, provide for children's education, and preserve your assets for retirement.

Just the Basics

There are four documents that at a minimum every person should have. These include: 1) Last Will and Testament; 2) Financial Power of Attorney; 3) Advanced Directive-Medical Power of Attorney; and 4) HIPAA Waiver and Privacy Release.

Last Will and Testament

What is a Will?

A Will is a document that describes how the maker of the Will wants his or her property distributed after his or her death. It is an instruction manual that guides the court as to how to distribute his or her assets. People make Wills because they want to decide who will receive their property, how much each person will receive, when they will own it, and in some cases what they can do with it. A Will has no effect during a person's lifetime.

What are the Benefits of a Will?

When you die without a Will, the state court through the **Intestate Probate** process will choose the administrator of your estate, a Guardian for your minor children, and distribute your assets according to the State's plan, not yours. The court will not consider your desires on how you want your assets distributed.

With the use of a Will, you can protect your family by making provisions to meet their present and future financial needs after you are gone. You can minimize taxes that might reduce the size of your estate. You can name the Executor or Personal Representative who will ensure that your wishes are followed and not that of the state's. You can name a Guardian for your minor children. You can establish trusts so that those who inherit who are minors or incapacitated can receive assets and have the assets managed for them. Most importantly, you can secure the peace of mind knowing that your family and other heirs will be taken care of according to your desires.

Who are the Players Involved in a Will?

There are several players involved in a Will, including the decedent, the heirs, and contingent beneficiaries. The person who dies is a decedent. When a person dies leaving a Will, he is said to have died testate. That means that the Will must be submitted to the court and the court will appoint an Executor named in the Will to see that the decedent's property is distributed according to her wishes. Heirs are the persons named in a Will who receive the assets of the decedent. Contingent beneficiaries receive the assets of the decedent if the Will provides that if an heir should predecease a decedent, then the contingent beneficiary is to take assets that would have gone to the heir.

Does a Will Avoid Probate?

No. A Will is a document that describes how the decedent wants property distributed after her death. In order to distribute the property, the Executor must file documents with the court, including the Will, and go through the Probate process before any distributions can be made to the heirs.

Probate is a public process that can follow one of two paths. First, a person can prepare a Will and the court will follow the instructions in the Will on distributing the decedent's property. Second, the person can fail to prepare a Will, and a Probate will be opened intestate, meaning that the state will determine who is to administer the decedent's assets, how they are to be distributed, and which claims are valid and to be paid out of the Probate.

Whether you have a Will or not, the process of distributing your assets, paying creditors, paying taxes and other expenses, will be a public process for all to see, and the expense of Probate will be deducted from the assets of the estate or paid by the heirs.

Do I Need to Name a Guardian for My Children?

Yes. In your Will you should nominate a Guardian for the children and a Conservator of the assets. Often this is done through the establishment of a minor child trust with a trustee to manage the assets and a Guardian to provide for the children's care until they reach maturity. One person can perform both functions, or you may name one individual as the Guardian and another as the Conservator or trustee.

For those parents who choose to leave their money and property to their children in trust, the assets are transferred to the trust upon death. A trust document states how you want the money to be spent, you name who the trustee is who will manage the assets and determine when the trust should terminate. A trust can terminate at any age, not automatically at the age of majority. The trustee, named in the trust, manages the trust assets and has the responsibility for paying for your children's living expenses, health, education, maintenance, and support.

Whether you are naming a Guardian, Conservator or a Trustee, you should name a backup individual in case circumstances prevent your Guardian or Conservator from performing their fiduciary duties. Once you've made the decision, you should also discuss the financial and child care arrangements with the Guardian, Conservator, and/or Trustee. You are placing a big responsibility on these people and you need to be sure that they are comfortable with the responsibility and that they are willing to accept the responsibility when you draft your Will.

What is a Spousal Share?

Most states have legislation requiring a certain percentage of assets be left to the spouse no matter what your Will says to do with your assets. In Oregon, the spousal elective share is a percentage of your assets which varies depending on the length of marriage. It is usually not a problem, because most people leave everything to their spouse on the first death. However, that is not always the case, and you need to be aware of any spousal elective share in your State. Further, the law could change the amount of the share at any time.

What Does an Executor Do?

You can choose anyone you want who is an adult and legally competent to serve as the Executor of your estate. Most people choose their spouse or a sibling as their Executor. However, the duties of the Executor in handling Probate are extensive, so you want to consider naming an individual who has the time and ability to handle the many tasks involved in Probate.

During Probate your Executor is required to collect and provide safekeeping for the estate's assets, notify all creditors and pay all valid debts, collect any sums owed by the estate, file for retirement benefits, Social Security and veteran benefits, manage the estate assets, sell assets as directed by the Will or required by state law to pay expenses or for distribution to heirs, keep detailed records of all estate transactions, distribute assets upon court order to the beneficiaries, file the decedent's final tax return, choose a tax year for the estate, file any estate income tax return, and prosecute or defend any litigation that arises during the Probate.

Will Substitutes that Reduce or Eliminate Probate

There are methods of holding title to property that can eliminate Probate for certain property, but they may not be able to replace a Will. Examples of options to avoid or reduce Probate include the use of living trusts, joint ownership, pay on death accounts, community property, joint-tenancy with right of survivorship, tenancy by the entirety and beneficiary designations on certain accounts.

Revocable Living Trust

In my experience a Revocable Living Trust is the most frequently used strategy by estate planning attorneys to protect your financial privacy and reduce the need for Probate. A Revocable Living Trust is a legal agreement in which you transfer your assets in trust to be managed by a trustee for the benefit of one or more people. Usually, each spouse will create their own trust for the benefit of the other spouse. In addition, quite often both spouses are co-trustees of each other's trust. The trusts are revocable, so at any time the trust may be dissolved by the person making the trust. Once assets are transferred to the trust, the trustee(s) are responsible for managing the trust assets.

While the Revocable Living Trust provides asset management, it does not provide asset protection. Creditors and others can go after assets in a revocable trust to satisfy a debt.

Your Revocable Living Trust is not a matter of public record. Further, the provisions of your revocable living trust provide for your trust to continue after your death for a short period of time while the assets in the trust at death will be transferred to beneficiaries or to other trusts and will escape Probate and the associated costs and publicity of Probate.

Just because you have a Revocable Living Trust does not mean that you will not have to go through Probate. If you fail to put any assets into the trust, and the assets do not transfer by means other than Probate, then those assets will go through Probate and be subject to creditor claims. To accomplish this limited Probate, a Pour Over Will must be provided in conjunction with your revocable living trust so that any assets that you have not added to the trust Will *pour over* into the trust and be managed as other trust assets. As long as you continue to place new assets into the trust during your lifetime, there may be no assets subject to the Pour over Will.

Joint Ownership for Non-Probate Assets

Property you and your spouse own jointly with right of survivorship will pass privately to your spouse outside of Probate at death. Using joint ownership for the family home and a modest bank account or brokerage account is a simple way for your family's life to go on while the Probate process might be occurring with respect to other assets. Joint ownership can also be set up with a non-spouse so that assets pass directly upon death. The disadvantage of using joint ownership is that it eliminates many of the planning techniques that can be used to defer or eliminate estate taxes or affect the distribution plan in your Will.

Pay on Death Account

A pay on death designation names a beneficiary to receive account balance at the time of the party's death. Financial institutions will recognize the pay on death designation and transfer those assets without the need to go through Probate.

Beneficiary Designations

Certain accounts such as life insurance policy proceeds, retirement plan benefits, annuities, and individual retirement accounts go directly to beneficiaries instead of passing through Probate. While the beneficiary designations can avoid Probate, they can also destroy the provisions of your Will and your intent as to how you want your assets distributed. For example, you have a 401(K) plan at your place of employment. You name your wife as the primary beneficiary and your oldest daughter as the contingent beneficiary. Your wife predeceases you and you don't change your 401(K) beneficiary designations. You draft a Will after your wife's premature death, leaving everything to your three children equally. You intend that your $400,000 401(K) account will be left to each of your children equally. However, your beneficiary designation on the account leaves everything to your oldest daughter. Who receives your 401 account? Your oldest daughter receives 100%. Beneficiary designations on an account will trump what distribution you have designated in your Will.

When drafting a Will, you must ensure that the terms of the beneficiary designation on life insurance policy proceeds, qualified retirement plans, annuities, and IRAs are in agreement with the designations in your Will.

Power of Attorney

What is a Power of Attorney?

A Power of Attorney is a document by which one person gives another person (the "attorney" or "agent") the power to conduct certain actions on his or her behalf. While called an "attorney," the person given the power is really any individual who you have elected to manage your financial affairs in the situation where you cannot handle your own affairs. The Power of Attorney can also be used for medical decisions as well as financial.

What are the Benefits of a Power of Attorney?

A Power of Attorney provides for someone else to make your financial decisions for you in situations such as when you are incapacitated, when you are hurt in an automobile accident and cannot deal with your financial affairs, for someone to conduct business matters for you while you are away, when you're in the hospital for illness, having a baby, undergoing surgery, while on vacation, or when you can't get to the bank or post office.

Situations Covered by a Power of Attorney

A Power of Attorney can be general or specifically limited. For example, a grandparent who is losing her eyesight may want her son to handle her bills, write checks to cover the bills because she can no longer see. A single mother may want to have someone designated as her attorney in case she develops some mental or physical disability. A husband and wife may want to give each other authority to manage the finances should either one become incapacitated.

Risk of a Power of Attorney

The major risk is that the attorney or agent will take advantage of the principal who gave them the authority to handle their financial affairs. Not all people are honest. There are situations where the agents or attorneys proved to be untrustworthy and stole money from the principal. Therefore, the person who is selected as the agent needs to be someone that you trust to fulfill the responsibilities stated in the Power of Attorney. It does not have to be a relative, but it needs to be someone trustworthy and financially responsible. Avoid relatives and friends who are inexperienced in financial matters, have difficulty managing their own money, have credit problems, or who have health issues.

What Decisions Can the Agent Make?

A Power of Attorney can be as broad or as limited as the principal desires. On the broadest scope, the principal can take any action allowed under Oregon law. On the other hand, a Power of Attorney can be limited to a specific transaction or for a specific time period.

In the Power of Attorney, just as an Executor for the Will, or the trustee for the trust, a principal may want to designate a successor agent to act on his or her behalf if the original agent is unable or declines to serve. The Power of Attorney document will spell out the powers granted to the successor agent.

When is a Power of Attorney Effective?

A Power of Attorney can be a **springing** power or it can be an **immediate** power. A Power of Attorney is effective when it is signed unless the Power of Attorney expressly states that it becomes effective at a future date or upon the occurrence of a future event. When a future event, such as incapacity of the principal, occurs and the Power of Attorney is triggered, this is referred to as a springing power. The Power of Attorney springs into existence upon the incapacity of the principal. One of the problems with a springing Power of Attorney is that it requires some mechanism to determine that the event has occurred. Just think of the awkwardness of a child having to get a doctor's certification that mom is incompetent to handle her financial affairs in order for the springing power to be triggered and for the child to take care of mom's financial affairs. On the other hand, as long as mom is competent she has no worry that agent or attorney will take advantage of her or spend her assets.

When a Power of Attorney is effective upon signing, it gives the agent the absolute authority to deal with the principal's assets the same as the principal. In most cases, for example where mom names her daughter as the agent under the Power of Attorney, there is no problem. However, not all daughters are trustworthy and it does expose mom to fraud and potential loss of assets.

When Does a Power of Attorney End?

A Power of Attorney is a living document that terminates upon the death of the principal. Usually when a Power of Attorney is drafted there is an express provision for termination. Frequently, terms for termination are death of the principal, divorce of the principal if the spouse has been named as the agent, and at any time it is revoked in writing by the principal.

Limited Power of Attorney

A Limited Power of Attorney is written so that the agent's power is limited to a specific transaction or event. A Limited Power of Attorney usually terminates when the purpose of the Power of Attorney is accomplished. A Limited Power of Attorney could also terminate if the agent dies, becomes incapacitated, or resigns. These uncertainties require you name a back-up agent.

Why Do I Need a Power of Attorney if I Have A Revocable Living Trust?

Just as assets outside the Trust pass to Probate, any assets that are not in use in conjunction with a Revocable Living Trust may be transferred to the Trust by use of a Pour over Will leaving everything to the trust.

While a revocable living trust is a document frequently used in planning, there are several different types of trusts used for different purposes that may be appropriate for your situation, such as a Marital or "A" trust, a Bypass or "B" trust, a Testamentary Trust, an Irrevocable Life Insurance Trust, a Charitable Trust, a Qualified Terminable Interest Property Trust, or a Grantor Retained Annuity Trust, just to name a few. Also, consideration should be given to whether you need a revocable trust or if an irrevocable trust which will reduce the amount subject to estate taxes by removing the value of the irrevocable trust assets from your estate is appropriate.

While one size does fit all, and there is no generic solution for each individual family, all estate planning starts with the four basic documents.

Properly planning your estate requires careful drafting, planning, and execution. Estate planning is a highly individualized, constantly changing, and legally complex procedure, and it is unlikely that if you utilize a kit purchased from the web, bookstore, or through mail promoters, or standard computer-generated document creation programs that you can provide appropriate documents for your unique family situation. This is one area where you should consult a professional to review the array of planning tools that can help you achieve your goals.

Advance Directive-Medical Power of Attorney and End of Life Directive

Don't put the burden on your family to make health care decisions without telling them what you want. The Oregon Advance Directive is a legal form that allows you to choose a health care representative. The person you select as your representative can make medical decisions for you whenever you're unable to speak for yourself. In selecting your medical representative, you want to select someone you can trust and someone who can make the medical decisions when you can't.

We often think of the need for serious medical decisions occurring at end of life, but the need to have an Advance Directive and someone making the decisions for you can occur at any time -- from an unexpected fall, from a skiing accident, from an auto accident, or from that unexpected heart attack.

Your doctor has determined that you've become incapacitated. What does he do to determine how to treat you in accordance with your intentions for medical treatment? You have had the foresight to prepare an Advance Medical Directive and appointed someone to make medical decisions for you. Once your doctor has determined that you're incapacitated, he will review your Advance Medical Directive, contact your medical representative, and discuss your condition with them.

There are two steps to planning for the time when you become incapacitated and cannot make medical decisions for yourself. First, complete an Oregon Advance Directive that identifies your choices for medical treatment. Second, discuss the Oregon Advance Directive with your medical representative, provide your representative with a copy of the Advance Directive, and discuss your feelings and intentions with respect to those end-of-life decisions addressed in your Oregon Advance Directive.

It is extremely difficult for family members and spouses to make decisions about life-prolonging care, limited care, and comfort care when the need might arise. By knowing your intentions in advance, that family member acting as a health care representative can make those decisions knowing that they are doing what you wanted them to do and that they don't have to make these very difficult decisions.

HIPAA Privacy Information Waiver and Release Authority

Plan in Advance for That Time When Circumstances Occur And Medical Providers Need to Provide Health Information with Others to Ensure that You Receive the Best Possible Medical Treatment

The Health Insurance Portability and Accountability Act ("HIPAA") privacy rule provides important privacy rights and protections with respect to the dissemination of your health information. While the Act is designed to ensure privacy protection to your medical information, there are times when it is necessary to share that health information to ensure that you receive the best treatment possible. As discussed above in the section on Advance Directive, one of those times is when your health representative has to make treatment decisions when you cannot.

HIPAA generally allows health care providers to communicate with a patient's family, friends, or other persons who are involved in the patient's care. If you are able to communicate, you may give permission to your medical providers to share relevant information with family members or others and give them an opportunity to agree or object to the treatment. Note that this communication extends only to a friend or family member who has been identified by the patient.

The HIPAA rules also apply to mental health information, with certain exceptions. One exception is for psychotherapy notes. Psychotherapy notes are defined by statute as notes recorded by a health care provider who a mental health professional documenting the contents of a conversation is doing a private session with a patient.

Having a HIPAA release ensures that your medical situation can be discussed with those individuals you have designated.

The HIPAA rules permit but do not require medical providers to disclose medical information. Medical providers can be subject to more stringent privacy standards under other laws. Because of these limitations, it is advisable to have a HIPAA release prepared in advance so that there's no question that a medical provider can discuss your medical condition with those you have designated, so that if necessary they can make informed medical decisions regarding your treatment when you cannot make those decisions.

CHAPTER 5

HOW TO PROTECT YOUR DIGITAL ASSETS

What are Digital Assets and Why Do You Need a Digital Estate Plan?

"What are digital assets, and do I have any?" is a common start to my conversations with potential clients or other estate planning professionals when I mention that my firm creates digital estate plans. We all have a lot more digital assets than what we realize. How about that bank account, email and credit card accounts? Here are some of the internet accounts that most of the people I work with have today. How many of these digital accounts do you have?

Can your Personal Representative handle these accounts when your die?

- Email;
- Photos;
- Linked In;
- Facebook
- ITunes;
- Online credit card accounts;
- Online bank accounts;
- Kindle;
- Software subscriptions;
- Cloud based storage values;
- Amazon account;
- 401 K account;
- Professional marketing accounts;
- Website administration access;
- Software subscriptions;
- Brokerage accounts;
- Instore;
- Twitter;
- Snapchat;
- Insurance accounts; and
- Cell phone account.

Once we start to list the internet accounts and applications the client has, the universal response is *"I never thought of that. I guess I need to plan how to handle these accounts when I die "*

Most People Have Never Thought About What Happens to Their Digital Accounts When They Die

Whether you are 18 or 88 you probably have online accounts. If you are like most people you haven't concerned yourself with what happens to your online accounts and storage when you die. While little thought has been given to these accounts prior to preparing and estate plan, when it is time to start your plan you now have to consider another quality and skill in the person you choose to handle your estate when you die, are they technologically savvy enough to deal with your digital library of online accounts? Especially for the baby boomer generation and later, many would be Executors would be lost trying to deal with computers and online technology.

Is digital planning important? Which is more important to you, losing something with a monetary value, or losing a lifetime of notes, cards, photos and things of sentimental value to your family. What if you lose a Facebook account with photos of your deceased loved one. This can be more traumatic than being unable to access a bank account. On the other hand, you survivor's not being able to access a bank account can be just as troublesome.

While most members of the millennial generation are just starting their careers and building their assets. They are digital smart and probably have more digital assets than any other generation. Planning at an early age may be more important to the current generation than it was to past generations. When we are young we don't imagine that we will die until we are retired and have lived a long life. But premature death happens. For example, that trip down the stairs, the fall in the bathroom, the automobile accident, the unexpected cancer. Regardless of age, some people want certain digital assets to be destroyed. Some may want their digital assets preserved. Some may want a combination of preservation and destruction. What you want is not going to happen unless you make your wishes known in your estate planning documents. No one knows how much data they will accumulate during their lifetime. Regardless of the quantity, if you want it treated in a certain way on your death or disability, you must put it in writing in a legal planning document.

Oregon Reacts to the Draconian Treatment of Account Information by Digital Providers

If you live in Oregon, there is a new Oregon law that addresses some of the issues related to handling digital assets. The Oregon version of the Revised Uniform Fiduciary Access to Digital Accounts Act ("Act") became effective January 1, 2017. The Act provides a means for your Executor/Personal Representative, your Power of Attorney agent or trustees of your trust to deal with your digital assists as long as this power is expressly stated in the document. If you fail to plan for your digital assets in your planning documents, then whatever terms and conditions you agreed to with your digital provider (bank, credit card company, google, face book, etc.) will control the handling of each digital asset. Some of these provider agreements allow them to delete all records and information when they are notified of a death. Getting things in order prior to death includes a list of internet accounts, user names, passwords and purpose of the internet accounts. By including your digital asset plan in your estate planning documents and the new law, you will have streamlined the ability of your Personal Representative to access and preserve your digital assets.

If You Fail to Plan There is a Risk That Your Digital Assets Will be Lost

Mary was always the family historian. She would take pictures at all of the children's birthday parties, her daughter's wedding, the soccer games, family vacations, the birth of her granddaughter and just about everything about the events of her extended family. One day, John, her husband got her a fancy iPad. She loaded in all her family photos so they would all be in one place. Then she found out she could store them on the cloud. She immediately loaded up all her photos, knowing that now they would never be lost. She could go to the cloud and share them with family on Facebook, and even print out copies. However, Mary had an unexpected heart attack and suddenly was gone. John had no idea what internet accounts Mary had, what her passwords were, or what information might be accessible on the internet. Without a digital estate plan for Mary's

Executor/Personal Representative to follow not only where the family photos at risk of being lost, but her other assets might not be identified or John might not be able to gain access. Further, these accounts could become the subject of identity theft, and create even more problems for Mary's family.

In most cases, lost digital assets will be of high sentimental value such as email, photos, videos, and social media posts. A majority of people from all generations have digital and internet assets with physical cash value as well, including online financial assets, online sales business, credit card reward points, published e-books, and domain names.

Does Your Personal Representative Have the Ability to Handle Digital Assets?

The ease with which we generate digital assets and use the internet leads us to believe that everyone is internet savvy and has the technical knowledge to obtain and secure our internet assets upon our death. This is far from the truth. The truth is that for every highly skilled technical person, there is an equally unskilled internet person. In naming a Personal Representative, Mary and John have to recognize the need for some computer/internet skills as well as honesty and responsibility in their Personal Representative.

Start Protecting Your Digital Asset Estate by Establishing a Digital Estate Plan Now Not Later

Unlike an estate plan for real property and monetary assets, a digital estate plan is important for everyone with internet accounts and digital assets. Planning for digital assets is done in your Will, Trust and Power of Attorney. In this age of smart phones, androids, iPads, laptops, tablets, and book readers, you need to spend time to create your digital estate plan. That plan will include discussing with you prospective Personal Representative his or her level of comfort with the internet and technology, make an inventory of your digital assets, and letting your Personal Representative know where to locate the inventory for when you pass. In your estate planning documents, provide for your Personal Representative to have the authority to access your digital accounts.

Make Sure Your Existing Will, Trust, and Power of Attorney Provides Express Authority to Control Your Digital Estate

Do you have an Estate Plan in place? If the answer is yes, now is the time to review your estate planning documents. If your documents were drafted ten or more years ago it is likely that your Will, Trust, and Durable Power of Attorney do not even address internet accounts. If your existing documents do not address internet accounts, update your documents now and provide for access to those accounts to the person(s) who will be handling your estate or making decision for you.

Organize Your Digital Asset Information Either Manually or Through a Protective Service

Organize your digital accounts, and let your Personal Representative or Power of Attorney know where this information is located. One method of protection is to make a list of all your passwords and accounts and store this information in a safe deposit box.

A second method is through the use of an encrypted password manager. With a password manager you keep all your digital and vital documents in one location with multiple layers of security. You create one very difficult to hack password rather than use easily memorable passwords, often using the same password across multiple accounts. Under either method you should change passwords frequently, and use a two-step authorization. Two of these password online secure storage options are **lastpass.com** and **dashlane.com.** This is not a recommendation. Do your due diligence in deciding which company if you use an online program, will handle your accounts and passwords.

Time to Update Your Estate Planning Documents?

How long ago was your Will or Trust created? If it was more than 5 years ago it was done at a time quite different with respect to the internet and social media. In fact, planning for digital assets may not have been considered when preparing your plan back them. If you have a plan that is at least 5 years old or if you need to get your physical estate and digital estate in order for the first time, then an experienced estate planning attorney can make things easier for your loved ones when you pass.

CHAPTER 6

CONTROL YOUR MEDICAL TREATMENT SO YOUR LOVED ONES DON'T HAVE TO MAKE HARD DECISIONS

Can You Plan Ahead What Treatment You Will Receive When You Have a Medical Emergency?

Everyone just assumes that when a member of your family is injured or disabled, that his or her medical provider will automatically provide access to medical records to you. However, in this litigious society, medical professionals are reluctant to provide family members access to a patient's medical records. In addition, medical personnel face stiff penalties for releasing private medical information. Because of the lock down on private health care information, you should have a special HIPAA Waiver and Release to ensure access to medical information. In Oregon, there is a statutory form of Advanced Care Directive that is inclusive of the medical information release. However, there is no assurance that if you are traveling to another part of the country and require emergency medical treatment, medical practitioners from another state will accept the Oregon form.

Plan Your Medical Treatment Like You Plan Your Wealth Transfer

In addition to needing access to your medical records, you should document your wishes for your future medical care. Either a Medical Durable Power of Attorney for Health Care or if you reside in Oregon, the Oregon Statutory Advance Care Directive provides the type of power to your agent. It gives the person you designate permission to make health care decisions on your behalf, if you are unable to do so in the future. When drafting your health care directive, you will express your wishes to your doctors as to many aspects of your medical care, including such factors as the use of life sustaining procedures. Generally, husbands and wives select each other as their health care agents to make the hard decisions for them.

Considerable time is spent on wealth transfer at death; not as much time is devoted to disability planning and planning for health care needs. Several years ago the nation's attention was drawn to *Terri Schiavo* of Florida who had suffered a brain injury and was receiving IV's and hydration for more than 10 years while she was in a vegetative state. Relatives, including her ex-husband, battled over whether or not to use life sustaining procedures. If Terri Schiavo had planned for the unexpected, living in a vegetative state, she could have made her wishes known and avoided the anguish and conflict among her family.

How Will You Pay for Your Care if You Can't Take Care of Yourself?

An Advance Health Care Directive is essential so that your loved ones don't have to go to court to make those hard decisions and try to determine what you would want them to do. In addition to having access to medical records and providing advance health care directives, part of your estate planning should be to provide for long term care and potential disability. Through the use of a Revocable Living Trust or Will, in combination with your Power of Attorney, you can provide for decisions if you become disabled. However, along with disability comes an enormous financial burden. Planning for those catastrophic situations of disability or the time when you and your spouse can no longer take care of yourselves, requires planning with your financial advisor.

Why You Fear Discussing Long Term Care with a Financial Advisor

We all fear that at some point we will either encounter disease, or simply be unable to take care of ourselves due to age, illness or injury. We dread the thought of giving up our independent lifestyle and taking care of our needs. A long term care facility is something few of us want to talk about. Many of us will likely need to consider long term care some time after age 65. Today there are many options for long term care. Those options include nursing homes, assisted living, continuing care communities, adult care centers, adult foster care, and of course home care. All of these options have one thing in common: they are very expensive. When you are working on your estate plan for disability, this is the time when you should bring in a financial planning advisor who can work with long term care insurance and design coverage plans to fit your budget. Long term care insurance reduces the depletion of household assets needed by the spouse or intended to be passed to future generations. Long term care insurance can provide the resources so that you can be taken care of, without reliance on your spouse, children or other relatives to provide care for you while taking care of their families. A private policy gives you better selection of facilities, such as nursing homes, adult day care, assisted living, adult foster care and home health care. In contrast, many government programs will not pay for assisted living and many assisted living facilities will not accept Medicaid patients. Many nursing homes also limit the number of Medicaid patients they will accept. While saving money, using Medicaid to pay for long term care can affect your quality of life.

You Cannot Afford To Procrastinate on Your Long Term Care Planning

Long term care insurance can't be purchased after you need it. It must be purchased before it is needed, and the younger you are when you purchase it, the lower the premiums will be. Though the premiums are lower when you are younger, most people consider purchasing long term care insurance when they are in their 50's or early 60's. To acquire long term care insurance you should work with a financial planner who can help you select the best policy to meet your needs and with premiums and benefits that fall within your budget. If you do not have or cannot acquire Long Term Care insurance, you need to address advanced planning strategies to help qualify for government assistance while preserving assets for your spouse.

There are Many Ways to Lose Your Retirement Savings; Don't Let Disability Be One of Them

In the recent economic downturn, many currently employed individuals have had their retirement plans changed due to a drastic reduction in their retirement savings. There are many stories of workers losing 35-50% of their retirement nest egg. In addition to poor investment returns, your retirement savings can be drained by an illness or injury that prevents you from working. If you suffer a disability, not only will your retirement nest egg quickly be depleted, but your immediate standard of living can be destroyed. There is a solution to this problem.

Disability insurance coverage is intended to be income replacement insurance. This type of insurance is needed while you are working and is designed to provide a benefit up to a certain percentage of your current income if you become disabled. Disability insurance has a number of variables which can be designed to meet your needs and at a premium that is within your budget.

Disability planning when you are working or after you are retired is an often overlooked aspect of estate planning. Not only do you have to assure that your medical records are accessible to those who can make decisions for you, that you have provided guidance to those who will make the hard decisions for you in case of a catastrophic illness, but that you have protected your family by considering long term care and disability insurance if you are still working.. As a part of your estate plan, you should not only speak with your estate planner, but also with a financial planner who can design an insurance plan for you so that you can decide whether the benefits outweigh the cost.

CHAPTER 7

ARE YOU WORKING FOR THE IRS? HOW TO SAVE TIME, TAXES AND STRESS

When You Die You Will Pay Taxes Again On Income That You Already Paid Taxes on When You Were Alive

It is often said that the only sure things in life are death and taxes. If you thought that a lot of your income was taken by taxes while you were alive just wait until you die.

While you were alive you most likely paid taxes for:

- Federal income tax;
- State income tax;
- FICA;
- Medicare;
- Sales tax;
- Gasoline tax;
- Utility tax;
- Vehicle fee tax;
- Telephone service tax;
- Driver's license fee;
- Dog license fee;
- Income tax of social security received; and
- Property tax.

The list of taxes paid while you were alive is probably longer, but that is all I could think of off the top of my head. Would you be surprised to learn that when you die you get to pay taxes again if you have not spent too much and have saved enough to exceed the federal and if you live in a decoupled state like Oregon, a state death tax?

In addition to the estate taxes, depending on how you left your assets, you may also owe a generation skipping tax, gift tax which you paid while you were alive, capital gains tax, federal income tax, and state income tax. It is understandable that regardless of the size of your estate when you die, a vital component of your planning will be to devise a plan that leaves more of your money to your children and your spouse than to the IRS and the state taxing authority such as the Oregon Department of Revenue.

As you can see, the IRS and the Oregon Department of Revenue tax wealth during your lifetime, when you transfer it at death and when you transfer wealth to any generation. Although estate planning has become temporarily simpler thanks to the current higher federal estate tax exemption, there is no guarantee that the higher exemption will be in effect when you die. Ask yourself, with a current $20 trillion deficit in the United States 2017 budget, and over $92 trillion in unfunded future liability, will taxes be higher or lower in the future? The federal and state government will have their poison tax arrows pointed at you, your spouse, your children, and your grandchildren.

Estate Taxes-Two Against One, Why You Lose

The first type of tax is the **Wealth Transfer Tax.** For residents of Oregon, that includes the federal estate tax, the federal gift tax, and the Oregon inheritance tax. Certain property is exempt from the tax depending on the year when you die. In 2017, the federal estate tax exemption is $5.49 million and the Oregon inheritance tax exemption is $1.0 million. This is the amount that can pass free of estate tax. The federal tax rate is 40% and the Oregon tax rate is 10%-16%. Many states have their own inheritance tax, but not all states tax you estate.

Federal Gift Tax Exclusion. In addition, in 2017, there is a $14,000 annual federal gift tax exclusion. The federal gift tax rate is 40%, paid by the person making the gift. The federal gift tax is based on the fair market value of the assets transferred. This annual federal gift tax exclusion is per Donee. If you have five children you could gift in 2017 $70,000, $14,000 to each child, gift tax-free. Valuing the assets transferred can be quite a challenge whether it is a lifetime gift or valued for your estate at the time of death. There are many instances of appraisal wars between individuals and the IRS or the Oregon Department of Revenue leading to prolonged litigation.

The Estate Tax Marital Deduction. This deduction allows the first spouse to transfer to surviving spouse an unlimited amount of assets free of both estate and gift taxes. Assets transferred to your spouse can pass outright in a marital trust. While this may defer estate taxes on the first death in a marriage, assets remaining with your spouse on his or her death with a value greater than the exemption amounts will be taxed at the second death. Passing everything to your spouse sounds like a good idea for the first to die, but it may not be the best plan for your overall estate plan.

What is the Value of Your Estate?

The value of your estate is everything you own at the time of your death. You might be surprised at how high the value of your estate is when you consider all your assets. If you think it is large now, consider how your savings and investments will grow over decades, plus add in the value of your house when it is paid off, and add the face value of your life insurance policy. When your asset values are added together, it is very easy for a couple to reach the Oregon threshold tax trigger. At times the federal tax trigger has been lower than Oregon's exemption and so it is wise to consider tax minimization strategies regardless of the current size of your estate.

Don't Refer to Your Granddaughter as the "Skip Person"

Some might think that you can avoid the tax by leaving your assets to your grandchildren instead of your children. There is a Generation Skipping Transfer Tax imposed on any transfer you make to what is called the "*skip person*" for the layman that your children or great grandchildren or even an unrelated person 37 ½ years younger than you. The government does not allow this transfer without imposing a tax. This applies mostly to large estates because the same exemption amount applies, but is a consideration if you plan on skipping a generation and leaving assets to grandchildren.

The **Generation Skipping Transfer Tax** is an additional tax to the estate and gift tax that applies to any transfers to a second generation. The tax is punitive because the tax is a flat tax at the highest estate and gift tax rate in effect at the time of transfer. In 2017, the federal tax rate is 40%. The generation skipping transfer tax also provides for certain exemptions like the gift and estate tax.

Try to Step Up the Basis in Appreciated Assets to Reduce the Capital Gains Tax

Capital Gains Taxes paid on resale of the property received by the person receiving the gift are not necessarily an estate planning issue, but with the recent increase in the capital gains tax rate, there is a greater effect on property you might transfer.

When you transfer gifts, you still have to consider the income that those gifts earned up to the time of transfer. You are not allowed an income tax deduction for gifts, unless the gift is made to a charity. The lucky person who received the gift is not taxed. Not sure how the government missed that chance to tax. For any gifts during your lifetime, the person who receives your gift will take over your tax basis and holding period. Thus, if you purchase a stock for $20 and give it to your son when it is worth $100, the tax basis consists of the original amount that you paid for it, $20. This is different for gifts made at the time of death for which certain recipient of those gifts may get a stepped up basis. For example, with gifts made to the proper recipients, in the above example, their tax basis would be $100 instead of $20. This step up basis effectively eliminates any gain if the assets are sold right after your death.

If You Earn It, They Will Tax It

Just prior to death, you may have some income which will be subject to income tax. A final income tax return must be filed by the Personal Representative or Executor of the estate before the estate can be closed. The income to be reported can include unpaid wages, dividends, interest, rents received on rental property, and payments received on money lent.

Using a Financial and Legal Advisor to Build and Keep Wealth

While there are both tax and non-tax reasons to do your disability and death transfer planning while you still can, the significance of taxes at both the state and federal level make it mandatory that you consult with a qualified estate planning attorney who can deal with both federal and Oregon taxes. Your financial advisor helped you create wealth, she should participate in developing an estate plan that will leave more to your spouse and children and less to the IRS and Department of Revenue.

How Much Do You Own?

The first step in determining what estate plan is best for you, is to determine what the IRS and the State of Oregon consider to be your assets. There are two broad categories that will be your assets at the time the government looks at the transfer taxes. First, the property you still own at the time of your death. Second, certain property transfers or gifts you made during your lifetime. For simplicity, we will concentrate on what the IRS considers to be your property at death.

How Much Do You Own with a Joint Tenancy?

The IRS has a much broader definition of property you own at death than what you might think you own at the time you die. For example, if you are married, you and your spouse may own property as joint tenants. As you probably guessed, one-half of the value of the assets owned in joint tenancy with your wife will be included in your estate.

It does not matter who paid for the house, how it was acquired, or who has made the monthly mortgage payments. As long as the joint tenant is your spouse, one-half of the value will be included in your estate at death. However, assume that you own a rental house with your sister, as joint tenants with right of survivorship. If you die before your sister, the full value of the rental house will be in your estate, not 50%. The only two exceptions are if you and your sister received the rental house by gift or inheritance or your sister furnished a portion of the funds used to acquire the property. Thus, you may think you own 50% of a rental property when in reality for tax purposes at death you own 100%.

I Thought Life Insurance Was Tax-Free -- Am I Wrong?

Life insurance policies are often as sold as being tax free. The reality is that the proceeds from an insurance policy will be included in your estate at death. However, as discussed elsewhere, if you do not have any incidents of ownership in the life insurance policy and the policy proceeds are not payable to your estate, then the proceeds will not be in your estate at death and not subject to the federal or state death tax.

Annuities may or may not be in your estate. If you own an annuity that is for a certain number of years in the form of a joint life survivor annuity, to the extent you contributed to the value that may be remaining after your death, then that value is part of your estate. On the other hand, if you have an annuity that terminates upon your death, the annuity is not included in your estate.

What if your parents left their estate in trust? Then you are the beneficiary of the trust and you receive income for your life, but you have no power to determine what happens to the principal of the trust at the time of your death. Usually, the trust assets would not be included in your estate. However, a common planning technique is to establish a QTIP trust where you or the income beneficiary of the trust of assets your spouse left to you in trust and you have elected to take a marital deduction with respect to this trust. When you die, the assets of the marital QTIP trust will be included in your estate.

Why Can't I Give It Away Tax Free?

If you have made any gifts of life insurance or transfers to trust within three years of the date of death, not only will those assets be pulled back into your estate at death, but the amount of any gift tax payable on any gift you made within three years of your death will also be included in your estate. The value of your assets is generally the fair market value of your assets as of the date of your death. Because of these added complexities, your Personal Representative should consult with an estate planning attorney and a financial consultant before making the election of the date of that valuation for that property.

More Choices for the Representative of Your Estate

When you die, both Oregon and the federal government will allow certain deductions. However, if you owe federal estate tax, your Representative will have to make an election between taking the deductions on the federal estate or Oregon inheritance tax return or the federal or Oregon income tax return. A separate election for Oregon tax purposes that is different from the federal estate tax return election may be necessary. Oregon allows separate elections, including those elections provided by the IRS, whether or not a federal tax return is filed. The Oregon elections are irrevocable. When a federal tax return is not required, you still have to file an Oregon return to obtain the Oregon elections.

Certain expenses will be incurred at the time of your death and those expenses are allowable deductions either on your federal estate tax return or federal income tax return. In addition, those deductions may be used on your state inheritance tax return or your state income tax return. Further, the election made by your Personal Representative for federal purposes does not have to be the same as the election for the Oregon purposes.

There are generally four types of expenses that qualify for a deduction. Those expenses are: (1) funeral expenses; (2) administration expenses, such as the cost of tax preparation, attorneys' fees, Executor fees, trustee fees, Probate costs, appraisal fees, and expenditures to maintain your estate property; (3) claims for ongoing expenses and debts, and other financial obligations; and (4) indebtedness secured on real estate you own at the time of your death. If there is no tax due at the time of your death, the decision is easy and your representative will deduct your expenses on the income tax return.

Unless the Executor of your Will or the trustee of your Trust are experienced in financial and tax matters, then it is imperative that upon your death, they contact appropriate professionals to take advantage of the tax saving opportunities available after your death. Tax returns are due nine months after your death. Therefore, the Executor or trustee must make these elections with professional advice quickly even though they are going through the grieving process.

Can't I Just Leave it All to My Wife and Avoid Taxes?

Not only will your Executor or Trustee be faced with a daunting array of different taxes to consider at the time of your death, but they will also be faced with an array of exemptions or deductions that may or may not apply to your estate. Some of the major exemptions or deductions that are available if you live in Oregon that include: (1) the federal Marital Deduction; (2) the federal Unified Credit; (3) the Oregon Unified Credit, (4) the Oregon Special Marital Property election; and (5) the Oregon Natural Resource Credit. If you live in a different state you will have different state tax rates and exemptions. In some states there is no inheritance or income tax. In addition, depending upon your specific circumstances, there are available other options for reducing the size of your estate and, therefore, the size of your tax obligation.

If You Are Married and the First to Die, the IRS Lets Your Family Pay Your Taxes Later Rather Than Earlier with a Marital Deduction for Lifetime and Death Transfers

The Internal Revenue Code provides for a marital deduction that allows unlimited lifetime and death transfers tax free from one spouse to another.

When the first spouse dies, this allows your estate to pass from husband to wife tax deferred. This is not a tax exemption, it is a tax deferment. Assuming the husband dies first, when the wife dies, whatever has been left to her tax free using the marital deduction and that she still has on her death, will be included in her estate and taxed before any remainder is distributed to your children or other beneficiaries.

At the federal level, in order to qualify for the marital deduction: (1) the husband must be survived by the wife or vice versa; (2) the property must pass from the husband to the wife or the wife to the husband depending on who dies first; (3) the property is included in the estate of the person who dies; and (4) the property can be transferred outright or by trust in what is known as a QTIP election.

In order for the QTIP election to qualify for the marital deduction: (1) the property must qualify for the marital deduction by being other than a terminal interest; and (2) the election must be made on the federal estate tax return.

The federal marital deduction is also available for gifts given outright to your spouse. In addition, gifts made in trust qualify for the marital deduction if your spouse has the absolute right to income from the trust for life and either has a general power of appointment over the property or makes a QTIP election when filing a gift tax return.

Can I Leave the Family Farm to My Kids Without Paying Taxes?

Oregon complicates the use of the Oregon marital deduction for individuals who have natural resource property. Under Oregon law, owners of natural resource property at the time of their death are entitled to a separate credit to the extent that they meet certain qualifications. Generally, natural resource property is farm property, forest property and property used in a fishing business. What is included in each of the definitions is clearly defined in the Oregon statutes. If property qualifies as natural resource property, the representative of the estate or the trustee has several options and can use 100% of the credit, a part of the credit, or elect not to use the credit. Under Oregon law, there are several requirements before an individual or entity can elect to take the Oregon Natural Resource Credit: (1) the value of the property eligible for the credit must equal at least 50% of the total adjusted gross estate; (2) the property must be transferred to a member of the family or to a registered domestic partner of the decedent; and (3) during the five of the last eight years prior to the decedent's death, the decedent, or a member of the decedent's family, must have used the credit eligible property for farm or forest purposes. Eligible property held in an entity, such as a corporation, partnership, limited liability company and trust qualify for the credit provided that at least one of the transferees "materially participates" in the enterprise based on an active management standard. Before making this election, a person has to be sure that the property will continued to be used as natural resource property for at least five of the eight years following the death of the decedent, or there is a tax recapture.

The Natural Resource Credit creates another problem for married couples who would like to elect the federal marital deduction. If the estate of one of the spouses in a marriage has died and he or she makes a federal QTIP election or takes a marital deduction election for eligible property for federal tax purposes, then he or she must make a marital deduction election rather than a natural resource credit election on her Oregon tax return even though the decedent's estate is eligible for the natural resource credit election. For the person who owns timberland or a farm in Oregon, this means that they can either take the natural resource tax credit or they must take a QTIP or marital deduction for the property.

Oregon Decoupling – Or How to Make Estate Planning More Complicated

Estate planning for Oregon residents is more complex than for states that are not decoupled from the federal estate tax system because couples must consider the federal estate tax unified credit, the Oregon inheritance tax exemption, the generation skipping tax exemption, the gift tax laws, the Oregon qualified property credit, the marital deduction, and the Oregon natural resource credit and develop a create and Estate Plan to minimize the overall tax at the time of the death of the each spouse. Porting is available under federal law, but not Oregon law.

The IRS and State Of Oregon Cannot Agree on What Can Be Transferred At Death Tax Free

Under current law, the IRS allows a certain amount of property to be transferred at death tax free. The federal estate tax exemption, known as the Unified Credit, defines the amount of assets you can transfer before you pay federal estate tax. The

Unified Credit amount changes from year to year. In 2009 it was $3.5 million, in 2011 it was $1.0 million and in 2016 it was $5.45 million. Currently, in 2017 it is **$5.49 million**. The amount goes up or down depending on the party affiliation of the current presidential administration. Since 2011 it has been higher and lower than the Oregon exemption amount.

The Oregon exemption amount has been **$1.0 million** for many years and there is no indication of change in the future. This creates a gap from what is known as the "decoupling" of federal estate tax from Oregon inheritance tax. The gap in 2017 is $4.49 million. The Oregon Special Marital Property election discussed above, allows the widow of the decedent to defer the tax on this property until she dies, but does not exempt the property from taxation. On the other hand, when a single person dies, inheritance taxes will have to be paid on any "gap" amount.

In summary, with proper planning and compliance with the requirements of the law, everyone can transfer $5.49 million of property free of federal estate tax and $1.0 million of property free of Oregon Inheritance Taxes. Estate planning is not an exact science because no one knows what year they will die, what the tax exemption limit will be in the year of death, or the value of their estate at the time of death, until death occurs. In addition, in Oregon there is a separate inheritance tax, separate from the federal estate tax.

Whether it's planning for life insurance, retirement plans or other assets, since the size of the estate will be unknown until the time of death, an estate plan has to consider the potential for federal and Oregon estate taxes. You have to consider where the funds will come from to pay those taxes and who will pay those taxes. While a plan may look good on paper, it has to be practical and provide the funding for taxes and expenses at the time of death.

Portability is Not for Everyone

Under the *American Taxpayer Relief Act of 2012*, a deceased spouse may make a "***portability election***" under Federal Estate Tax Law. The effect of portability is that any unused federal exemption from the estate tax may be transferred to the surviving spouse and used at the time of his or her death.

The federal exemption in 2017 is **$5.49 million**. Portability is most useful when a married couple's combined estate value is in excess of a single federal exemption of **$5.49 million,** but less than two times the federal exemption of **$10.98 million**. In addition, portability might be a good planning strategy is if the marital property consists of items such as annuities, retirement plan accounts, and a personal residence. The advantage of portability is that it provides a double income tax savings because of the cost basis step-up at the death of the first spouse and then again at the death of the second spouse. Further, under certain situations it can simplify the estate plan by leaving all property to the surviving spouse. Another advantage is that retirement accounts, which can be rolled over to the surviving spouse, are protected from estate tax by the unused exclusion amount and still preserve the option to stretch the IRA distributions to children and grandchildren.

However, all is not good with portability. First, there is no adjustment for inflation for the unused portion of the federal exemption for the first to die. Thus, as assets increase in value, the increased amount may be subject to federal estate tax.

Second, there is a federal generation-skipping tax for gifts to grandchildren. The generation-skipping tax cannot be allocated to the exemption amount that is not used. Thus, property passing to grandchildren in excess of the surviving spouse's exemption will be subject to generational-skipping tax.

Third, if the surviving spouse remarries and his or her new spouse dies before the surviving spouse, the unused exemption amount will terminate.

Unless your estate approaches the federal exemption limit in value, **$5.49 million** in 2017, your use of the federal portability election is probably not the best option. The decision to use portability not only requires an analysis of tax factors, but consideration should be given to such non-tax factors as the age and health of the surviving spouse, the likelihood of appreciation of remaining assets, the likelihood of a significant inheritance by the remaining spouse, and whether or not the surviving spouse is likely to remarry. In most cases, the tax factors will be given more weight and you should choose the strategy that yields the lowest tax.

CHAPTER 8

GIFTING -- ONE SIZE DOES NOT FIT ALL

Every estate plan is unique and should be customized to your particular values, personality, family relationships, asset values, and goals. An estate planner, like a NASCAR race car team, has a toolbox of techniques and strategies that can be applied to specific circumstances. Further, if the size of an estate justifies it, an estate planner can get an advanced opinion from the IRS. What follows is a non-exclusive description of strategies and techniques available to increase the share of your estate going to your family and reduce the portion of your estate going to the IRS.

Christmas Comes Every Year

Everyone is allowed to give to as many individuals as you wish tax free, up to the $14,000 per year in 2017 per Donee. If you have a large family with five children and five grandchildren, this means you can give away up to $140,000 per year. Assuming an average 40% federal estate tax rate and that the estate value exceeds the exemption amount that would save you $56,000 in estate tax when you die. If you are married, you and your spouse can each make annual gifts of $14,000 per Donee. That would double the total amount that the above individual could give to children and grandchildren.

Although you and your spouse can give away $28,000 for each Donee tax free each year, you may have concerns with outright gifts because you lose control over the property. Before making your annual gifts, you need to determine if there are any issues with the Donee that might put the gift in jeopardy, such as bankruptcy, creditor problems, potential divorce, addiction, or financial immaturity. You also have to consider your future income needs. Do you have enough cash flow if there is an economic downturn?

By having an annual gifting program within the annual tax free limit, you avoid gift tax, the Donee do not pay income tax, the annual gift does not reduce your lifetime exemption, and at death, and you save about 40% in estate tax.

Give the Gift of Health and Education

In addition to the annual gift exclusion amount, you can also take advantage of the unlimited gift tax exclusion. To take advantage of the health and education exemption you must follow the rules. For example, any payments for medical expenses or educational expenses must be made directly to the provider in or to qualify. There are no exceptions, regardless of your relationship to the person who benefits, your payments must be made directly to the medical or educational provider. What qualifies as educational expenses? Qualifying educational expenses include tuition. However, they do not cover items most people would think they would cover such as books, dormitory fees, board or other similar expenses. Qualifying medical expenses include payments directly to the provider for diagnosis, cure, mitigation, treatment or prevention of disease. You can also get credit if you pay a provider for a procedure that affects a structure or bodily function that is also essential for medical care. I have seen this used for death bed planning by prepaying a loved one's tuition cost. The qualified medical and educational gifting exclusion is in addition to and does not replace the annual exclusion for gifts.

Where You Live When You Die Does Make a Difference, Credits and Marriage

In Oregon, when the first spouse dies, if certain rules are followed, then a husband may pass to his wife, or vice versa depending on who dies first, an unlimited amount of lifetime and testamentary assets tax deferred. To qualify for the federal marital deduction, the property must be in the decedent's estate, the decedent must be survived by his spouse. Only a property interest that passes or has passed from the decedent to the surviving spouse is entitled to the deduction and the property cannot be a non-deductible terminal interest. Qualification for the Oregon special marital property deduction is similar to the federal requirements. The property interest may pass by outright gift, by will, by trust, under the intestate laws, by gifts during the during the decedent's life or by transfer of jointly held property with the surviving spouse. To avoid the terminal interest rule, property may be passed by life estate with the power of appointment, a QTIP trust, or an estate trust.

When the first spouse dies, any property transferred would first be elected to be part of the Unified Credit of the deceased spouse, which is a true deduction. To the extent the decedent's property exceeds the Unified Credit limit, then the decedent's representative will elect the Marital Deduction which will pass assets to the surviving spouse without tax at that time. However, the assets passed to the spouse at the first death will be included in the surviving spouse's estate. The tax is only deferred, not avoided in total, because when the surviving spouse dies and the assets are passed onto the children they will be subject to an estate tax. From a federal prospective, the current exemption amount in 2017 is high, $5.49 million per person and with portability, for many families does not create a federal tax problem. However, the Oregon exemption amount is on $1.0 million and there is no portability. Further complicating the problem is that we have no idea what the tax rate or exemption amount will be in the year that you die. Thus, we have to plan with a protective wall in case of tax consequences.

Credits, Exemptions, Exclusions, Deductions, Deferments- Use All of Them to Minimize Your Taxes

If you are married and your combined estate with your spouse exceeds the Oregon and the federal Unified Credit amount, one alternative is to use your lifetime exemption amount. With respect to the federal exemption amount, you can use it while you are alive or upon your death. On the other hand, the Oregon special property election is available only upon your death.

While you are alive, in addition to your annual $14,000 gift exclusion per Donee, you can transfer property equal to your lifetime unified exemption without paying federal gift tax. However, by transferring gifts during your lifetime, you will use up your unified credit that can be applied at the time of death. The advantage to gifting up to your unified credit limit during your life is that if you transfer an appreciating asset, such as rental real estate, the appreciation on the gifted real estate will not be a part of your estate when you die. Thus, the current value of the real estate is applied against your uniform credit, while if you wait to transfer the real estate until the date of death, the fully appreciated value will be applied against your unified credit. This could save you in taxes approximately 40% of the value of the real estate at the time of your death. However, by transferring the asset while you are alive the recipient will not receive a stepped up tax basis. If you beneficiary wants to sell the property shortly after your death, she could be hit with a significant capital gains tax. It should be noted that Oregon does not have a gift tax, but its death tax starts at a much lower level.

One of the most popular strategies used is a combination of a Credit Shelter Trust with a Marital Trust which usually provide you with the maximum exemption when you pass your assets onto your spouse or children. The special account for the federal credit is placed in a trust identified as a Credit Shelter Trust, a Credit Bypass Trust, a Family Trust or a B Trust. If your spouse is a non-citizen, there are limitations on the marital deduction. This discussion will assume that your spouse is a citizen. Note that under the introduction of federal portability and the increased capital gains tax, use of a Credit Shelter Trust may not be the best planning alternative in each case. In states that are decoupled with a lower tax trigger threshold, it is probably still a good planning strategy.

In order to take full advantage of the unified credit and the marital deduction in the estate plan, in non-community property states such as Oregon, a married couple should usually try to equalize their assets in their individual names. Avoiding assets passing by the right of survivorship, will allow for transfer of assets into the Bypass and Marital trust upon the first death, and will reduce the size of the husband's and wife's estate to avoid the rich spouse, poor spouse dilemma.

Using this technique, a married couple should be able to use the entire amount of the Unified Credit and limit assets in the Marital Trust upon the second spouse's death to minimize federal taxes.

Generally, a similar technique is available at the state level in Oregon. However, for Oregon, the Unified credit amount in 2017 is $1.0 million and the gap between the state credit of $1 million and the federal $5.49 million credit must be identified and elected on the tax return as an Oregon special marital property election. Oregon allows a separate QTIP trust for the state marital property in addition to the federal marital QTIP trust. The application of the Unified credit and Marital QTIP trust in Oregon follows the same pattern as the federal Bypass Trust and Marital Trust with the exception that the Oregon unified credit is lower and the Oregon inheritance tax rates range from approximately 10% to 16% instead of the 40% federal estate tax.

Give Away Your Home's Future Appreciation Now— The QPRT Solution

Whether both the husband and wife are alive, or there is only the surviving spouse, one option to reduce estate taxes is to put your personal residence in a trust and rent the residence back from the trust. In technical language, planners call this a qualified personal resident trust ("QPRT"), which is an irrevocable trust in which the grantor, either the husband, the wife or the husband and wife if are both alive, contribute the personal residence to the trust and in return receive the right to use the personal residence for a term of years. This is a gift subject to gift tax.

However, the government allows you to discount the value of the gift because as the husband and/or wife, you have retained the right to live in the personal residence for a term of years. Assume that you have placed your residence in trust and that the term of years is 15 years. At the end of the 15 years, the trust property passes to the beneficiaries of the trust, which are usually the children of the husband and wife.

If you out live the term of the trust, you win. If you do not survive to the end of the term of the trust, you lose, and the personal residence is included in your estate for tax purposes.

Assume that you out live the term of the trust, then where do you live? If you out live the term of the trust, you can then rent the residence at fair market rental value from the beneficiaries. The rent passes through the trust to your beneficiaries. To maintain control, you may name yourself as a trustee of the trust during the term and, therefore, you are able to make all decisions regarding your residence. Because of this tax advantage, the IRS is strict in the qualifications for a personal residence trust. In addition to only being applicable to a personal residence and retaining the right to use the personal residence for a certain period of time, the trust agreement must also require any income of the trust to be distributed at least annually to the settlor. In addition, the trust may also permit the addition of cash to the trust to be held in a separate account for trust expenses, such as mortgage payments, property taxes, and improvements. The trust is prohibited from holding any assets, other than one personal residence. However, under a QPRT, the trustee can hold limited amounts of cash to pay authorized expenses.

Under Oregon law, the capital gains tax exclusion for a personal residence should be applicable to the proceeds if the residence is sold. However, if at the end of the term the house is transferred to his children by way of a QPRT, the basis in the house will be the same for the children as it was for the parents. The children would not get the benefit of a step up basis.

At the beginning of the QPRT, the IRS will treat the contribution of the personal residence as a gift. However, to the extent that the value is less than a lifetime exclusion amount, the value of the gift will not require payment of a gift tax. Further, because husband and/or wife has an interest in using the home for a specified term, the IRS will allow the house to have a discounted value when gifted to the trust.

A QPRT can be a valuable tool to enable a couple to stay in their house, while transferring their home to the children without paying estate tax. But remember, one size does not fit all and before using a QPRT, you must consider the size of the estate, the age and life expectancy of the parents, the health of the parents, and the relationship with the children. QPRTs are discussed in more detail in the chapter under *Staying in Your Home in*

Retirement where its use for non-tax reasons are discussed in full.

IS and SCIN Can Save You Taxes If Your Children Are Good Credit Risks

To the extent that you own an appreciating property and have a need for income during your later years, the technique of selling the appreciating property through an installment sale (IS), with the self-canceling installment note (SCIN) to your children can reduce both gift and estate taxes. This technique can work when both parents are alive or when only a single parent is alive. The benefit of using this technique when there is only a single parent is that the surviving spouse has received a 100% step up basis for any appreciating property. Thus, when the surviving spouse sells the property with an installment note to her children, there should not be recognition of capital gains. However, this method is not firmly established and there are differences of opinions among tax practitioners whether or not the accrued gain on the assets would need to be recognized at the time when the installment note is canceled.

If you utilize this technique, you must make a sale for full and adequate consideration in order to avoid gift tax consequences. The transaction must be adequately documented and the principal amount of the installment note must be equivalent to the fair market value of the property being sold. Because this is usually done to generate income for the parent(s) and to minimize gift and estate taxes when the asset is transferred to the children, the parent(s) must be comfortable with the credit risk of the children. The income stream to the parents is a major purpose of this technique. An installment sale is a good way for parents to remove assets from their estate and transfer them to their children, but to the extent that the installment note has not been paid off when the parents die, the remaining balance is added to the parents' estate. Once it is in the parents' estate, it would be includable for both federal and Oregon estate tax purposes. The solution is to make the note a self-canceling installment note that is canceled upon the death of the parent(s). Because there is a likelihood that the note will never be paid off, a risk premium is added to the promissory note, either by increasing the principal or by increasing the interest rate above the applicable federal rate. A note that may not be paid in full requires this premium to meet the requirements to avoid a gift tax.

Private Annuities are Another Option

Private annuities are very similar to the installment sale with a self-canceling note technique previously described. With a private annuity, there is a sale of property in exchange for a privately issued unsecured annuity contract for which payments are made to the seller usually for his life. Annuities can be private or commercial.

As an estate planning tool, the value of property sold for the private annuity is removed from the seller's gross estate. As a result of the transfer, any appreciation is now outside of the seller's estate. At the seller's death, the annuity obligation terminates and the property, which is the subject of the annuity, is not in the decedent's estate. In effect, the appreciation on the property has been transferred without gift tax or immediate income tax consequences to parents, to children or to other beneficiaries. Under the Internal Revenue Code, the terms of the annuity are based on the seller's life expectancy.

Gifting FLPs and the Family Business, Who Is In Charge?

Doctors, Dentists, CPAs, Attorneys and Other High Risk Professions Have Used Family Limited Partnerships (FLP) for Both Asset Protection and Estate Tax Planning Purposes

For years business owners, doctors, dentists, CPAs, attorneys and other high risk professions have used family limited partnerships (FLP) for both asset protection and estate tax planning purposes. Although most professionals have to practice in professional entities, they can use limited partnerships or limited liability companies for their non-professional operations and their non-practice assets. Family limited partnerships are especially useful when used with other entities such as limited liability companies, and corporations.

The Family Limited Partnership as a Holding Company

For operational purposes, the FLP is often used as a holding company. The FLP will hold limited assets, but will hold interest in other companies or even a trust. A FLP's income is taxed to the partners. Thus, it avoids the double taxation of a C corporation.

A FLP will have a general partner and multiple limited partners. The limited partners have no or very limited management rights and are not liable for partnership debts beyond their partnership interest.

Remedies are Often Limited in Most States to a Charging Order Against the Partner's Partnership Interest

What is a Charging Order? A creditor who has obtained a judgment would seek a Charging Order against the debtor partner's interest. The Charging Order would order the general partner to pay over the debtor's partner's interest in any distributions from the partnership to the creditor. Thus, anything to be paid to the debtor partner would go to the creditor until the judgment is paid.

What can be done with the Charging Order is determined by state law. Some states allow foreclosure on the partnership interest and others do not. If the partnership interest cannot be foreclosed, to the extent there are no distributions to the partner, his or her assets have been protected from the judgment creditor. However, the charging order is not always the only remedy. To provide asset protection, each situation must be reviewed to determine who holds the interest. Sometimes, the choices are limited in a professional entity often required by law for professionals such as doctors, dentist, and attorneys.

Based on the goals and objectives for each situation, the ownership interest can be held by spouses, children or a trust. While the professional will be liable for any malpractice claims, as to other operations and assets, choice of ownership can be crucial. First, to the extent possible you do not want an interest in your name, because of the Charging Order and the creditor's ability to foreclose on it. Second, using a Trust provides some asset protection, while retaining flexibility. Third, ownership by the children would provide asset protection because the limited partnership interest would not only be the largest portion of partnership assets, but would not be in the parents name and subject to attachment. However, the gift to the children could create a gift tax liability, and the bulk of the partnership assets are controlled by the children. Further, the children's interest is subject to their liability and satisfaction of judgments against them. Finally, ownership by the children requires in many cases an irrevocable gift to take advantage of both asset protection and estate tax planning savings.

Tax Benefits of a Family Limited Partnership

A FLP can provide income tax benefits by moving income from high marginal tax rate parents, a doctor, dentist or attorney, to a lower marginal income tax rate of a child. The easiest example is when investment income is $100,000 in the partnership. If the marginal tax rates for the parents and children are 25% and 15% respectfully, the next tax is reduced by $10,000 per year. Further, the parents could reduce taxes further, by determining the distributions each year.

FLPs are often used in estate planning to minimize or even eliminate federal estate taxes and state inheritance taxes. Currently, the federal estate tax above the exemption is 40% and the Oregon inheritance tax starts at 10%. While there are exempted amounts before the taxes are triggered, those exemptions amount at the federal level have a history of being a political football to be kicked around by which ever party is in office. The individual federal exemption in 2017 is $5.49 million with an estate tax rate of 40%. Under Hillary Clinton, she would have reduced the exemption to $3.5 million and increased the tax rate to 45%. She never addressed the issue of portability which currently allows the surviving spouse to use the unused portion of the first spouse's exemption amount. President Trump promised to eliminate the federal estate tax- stay tuned.

Discounts Allow Estate Tax Planning and Keep Assets in the Family That Would Otherwise be Lost to Estate Taxes

The following discussion is based on current law at the time of publishing this book. The IRS has proposed regulations that would limit or eliminate the use of discounts for the FLP and FLC.

Under current IRS regulation, rulings and court cases, the value of a gift of a limited partnership interest can be reduced for two discounts: 1) a discount for lack of marketability; and 2) a discount for the lack of control with the limited partnership interest. The amount of the discounts taken has varied but discounts in the range of 30% are common. Thus, if parents gift assets in a FLP worth $2.0 million, the gift would be valued at $1.4 million. Using both the lifetime gifting exemption and the annual gifting exemption (currently $14,000 per Donee), over a few years of gifting, parents could maintain management over assets, transferred to their children, at a reduce value with a corresponding reduction in estate taxes. Not only does this save on estate taxes, but moves future appreciation from the parents to the children, saving even more on estate taxes. The IRS has just issued new regulations which could eliminate the marketability and minority FLP discounts as an estate tax planning tool.

Disadvantages to a Family Limited Partnership or LLC

There are many advantages to the family limited partnership, but some of the disadvantages include the administrative expenses of maintaining the partnership and the cost of an appraisal to determine discounted value, potential family disharmony, restrictive income tax rules, uncertain estate tax implications and maintenance of partnership formalities. In addition, one of the most significant disadvantages is that when a highly appreciated property is gifted to your children or other family members. There may be capital gain taxes that would have been avoided if the assets were transferred at the parent's death, rather than gifted during his lifetime.

In addition, both family limited family partnerships and family limited liability companies are coming under increased IRS scrutiny and actions taken within the family limited partnership, such as valuations for minority interest or lack of marketability discounts will more likely be challenged by the IRS in the future.

New Proposed Regulation to Curb Use of Estate Tax Valuation Discounts for Operating and Family Businesses

On August 2, 2016 the Treasury released proposed regulations that will drastically change the way professionals, business owners, and high net worth individuals do their estate planning. The new regulations severely limit the use of marketability and minority discounts. The Treasury considers the discounts a tax loop hold which it is closing. The regulations are proposed and will not become final until at least after a hearing on the proposals that took place in early December 2016. However, if you are a professional, business owner or affected individual, you should be aware of the pending changes.

The Proposed Changes That Could Eliminate Valuation Discounts and Disrupt Your Existing Estate Plan

In a nutshell, here are the significant provisions of the new regulations.

- Provide for a claw back period for any lapse of rights for transfers made within three years of death of the partner, eliminating the discounts for any transaction within the three year period;
- Eliminate any discount for transfers to an assignee;
- Disregard the ability of most nonfamily member owners to block the removal of covered restrictions except under certain conditions;
- Disregard restrictions on liquidation that are not mandated by federal or state law in determining the fair market value of the transferred interest; and
- Confirms that the regulations apply to limited partnerships, limited liability companies, corporations and partnerships.

What Do the New Regulations Mean to Doctors, Dentist, Attorneys and Business Owners?

Remember, as of this writing these regulations are only proposed, not final. However, assuming they become final the effect will be to eliminate the FLP discounts as an estate tax minimization technique. The taxes paid by partners when transferring their interest, will increase and may require the estate to sell assets to pay the taxes.

If You Own a Partnership Interest in an FLP You May Want to Make the Interest Transfers Now Before the Regulations Become Final-The Three Year Claw Back Rule

If use of the discounts was part of your estate planning strategy, you may want to consider making the transfer before the regulations are final. However, even that may not protect you. There is a three year claw back period from the date of death. If you make the transfer and die within three years, the new regulation would control the value of the gift.

While the proposed regulation is probably going to receive a lot of comment and some challenges, now is a good time to review your existing planning documents and operating agreements, to determine if immediate action is appropriate. If you are professional, business owner or high net worth individual, and do not have an estate plan in place now is the time to look at your options. You need to know the current value of your business and how to plan under the current rules before the changes are implemented.

Death Insurance-We All Need It, but Don't Make the IRS Your Biggest Beneficiary

Death Insurance, or as most people call it, Life Insurance, is a technique that can overcome the significant taxes that can be incurred for transfers made at death of the husband and wife. When couples initially discuss their estate plans with me, many shocked looks occur when they find out that the life insurance is not tax free. Life insurance agents have sold life insurance for decades with the understanding that the proceeds from the life insurance policy are tax free. While this may be true with respect to income tax provisions, it is not necessarily true with respect to other types of taxes.

An entire chapter, *Don't Make Uncle Sam the Beneficiary of Your Life Insurance,* is devoted to the use of life insurance as a planning technique. Life insurance can not only be used to pay expenses at the time of death, but also to pay taxes due on the transfer of assets at death. The use of life insurance and proper planning with life insurance is so important that I have devoted an entire chapter to the use of life insurance as a planning technique.

The IRA Stretch, Avoid the Tax Spiral That Will Shock You and Your Family

For many of today's baby boomers, individual retirement accounts, 401K, 403B and 457 plans and other qualified pension plans are the types of assets that make up the majority of their estate. Retirement plan assets require special attention when you are planning your estate. The rules are many and complex. If you fail to follow the rules, you can have a never ending spiral of taxes which could reduce your retirement plan assets by as much as 70%! Retirement plans are so important and so complex that I devoted a separate chapter to planning your transfer of your qualified retirement plans, other relatives, they do not receive the step up in basis. Therefore, there may be capital gain taxes that would have been avoided if the assets were transferred at the parent's death, rather than gifted during his lifetime. For a full discussion of retirement plans, estate planning strategies see the chapter, *"Stretching is Good, Avoid Reducing Your Retirement Benefits by Using This Strategy and Be Loved for Generations."*

CHAPTER 9

FAMILY HARMONY THROUGH ESTATE PLANNING AND SELECTING THE RIGHT PEOPLE TO MAKE DECISIONS

PROTECTING YOUR WIFE OR HUSBAND-- DON'T LET YOUR LACK OF PLAN TORMENT THEM

Create Stress and Conflict by Failing to Plan

If you failed to obtain a Pre-Marital or Post Marital agreement to maintain separate assets, spouses in a blended marriage comingle assets, and name each other as beneficiaries on their 401K, pensions, and life insurance policy. Commingling coupled with a failure to plan can lead to a life of torment for your surviving spouse and a division of your family that you never imagined. Issues that frequently create problems for the surviving spouse include his or her inability to manage finances; arguments among your children over control if you become disabled; pressure from your children toward mom to handle things differently, and strife between your children from a prior marriage, your wife's children from your prior marriage and children from the existing marriage. Worse yet, if you pre-deceased your new spouse, you may disinherit your children. With proper planning, all of these situations can be resolved through the use of very simple estate planning techniques such as a Power of Attorney, a Revocable Living Trust, specific instructions for determination of incapacity, and the appointment of an independent trustee with a living trust.

Is Blood Thicker Than Water?

There are many hard decisions for you to think about to preserve your assets for your family and maintain family harmony. For example, who is better to manage the money that you leave to your spouse once you have passed away--an independent trustee or your children? We all like to think of our children as being very competent and fair, and you probably have a hard time imagining your children taking advantage of your wife after you have passed away. However, when you think about it, your children have an interest adverse to your surviving spouse.

Whatever your surviving spouse spends takes away from what is left for your children when she passes away. She is put in an inherent conflict with your children. Whatever your spouse does, she is in conflict with your children. Your children's interest is to preserve your estate and to have as much of it passed to them on your spouse's death as possible. Your spouse will have her own needs and need income, and perhaps some of the principal from the assets you have left to her to live on without your sources of income after you have passed away. Absent a plan, there will be constant pressure for your spouse to provide an early inheritance to your children for things like a down payment on a house, a new car, tuition, a trip or home improvements. On the other hand, every time your spouse does a home improvement, takes a trip, purchases a new car or does something for herself, your children will be critical of her spending.

Have You Thought About Your Surviving Spouse Becoming Disabled?

Another life event that may come to your family after you have passed is your spouse's disability. Once your spouse becomes incapacitated, there will be a natural struggle among your children to control the family assets, minimize care for your spouse and preserve assets for the children. Absent planning, a court action will be required to establish your spouse's incapacity. Prepare for a prolonged battle in court with the children to determine who should care for your spouse and manage the family finances.

How to Disinherit Your Children Without Really Trying-The Second Marriage Problem

It is common today for many people to be married more than once. If you and/or your spouse have been married before and have children from the prior marriages and children from the current marriage, your spouse's idea of being fair to the children may be different from your idea. In fact, if your spouse has control over the assets because you failed to plan, your natural born children may be disinherited. In addition, after your death your spouse may remarry. Your estate may be drained by a new gold digging spouse or your spouse may be convinced to leave everything to her new husband when she passes away, effectively disinheriting your children.

No Single Solution – Planning and Communication Can Preserve Harmony

All of these potential problems can be reduced or eliminated. Working with an experienced estate planning attorney you can select t a few effective estate planning tools and strategies including a Power of Attorney, a living trust designed as A-B trust, with provisions within the trust specifically defining what is required for incapacity, and the use of either co-trustees or an independent trustee to manage the trust assets. While all of these conflicts are serious, a second marriage situation is ripe for creating major problems.

Often when a couple comes into the office, their first goal

stated is that they want a simple will naming each other as the sole beneficiary. If that is the extent of their estate plan, the children will receive nothing at your death, unless your spouse chooses to make a gift to them. Following your death, your spouse then remarries. If your surviving spouse then dies without a Will or made a Will transferring everything to her spouse, the assets are transferred to the new spouse leaving your children disinherited from any portion of the inheritance that you had intended them to receive. For most people, this is not their desired result. However, most people want not only to provide for their spouse if he or she survives them, but they also want to provide for their children when their spouse dies. Transferring half of your assets to your children upon your death does not solve the problem because your spouse may need that half of the estate to live on after you have passed away. Transferring all of your estate to your spouse creates a problem that your children may never see your inheritance. By using a sophisticated planning device known as a QTIP Trust you can usually solve most of the above problems.

QTIP to the Rescue – Putting Strings on Your Property

A QTIP trust is a special form of trust authorized by the Internal Revenue Code. This trust qualifies for a marital deduction and avoids state tax at the first spouse's death, and you can transfer your property to the QTIP Trust which allows you to separate your property into two shares. The first share is the income generated by the property and the other share is the property itself, or the principal. By separating your property into the two shares, you direct that each share goes to a different person. As long as the QTIP trust directs that all of the income goes to your spouse during her lifetime, it will qualify for the marital deduction. The principal can either be distributed to your spouse as needed, or it can all be preserved and distributed to your children following your spouse's death without an estate tax being imposed. You may not understand how a QTIP works, but properly drafted it should minimize the second marriage problem.

CHAPTER 10

FAIR OR EQUAL, IS THERE A DIFFERENCE? DIVIDE YOUR PROPERTY NOT YOUR FAMILY

When clients come to my office, they often have two goals in mind. First, they want their children to be treated equally. Clients tend to equate "equally" with "fair." Second, they want family harmony among their children. While the goals are well-intentioned, the goals are often incompatible and may create resentment among children who feel mistreated because one child may think she is entitled to more because she cared for elderly parents or contributed more financially to their parents' expenses.

When people think of estate planning, they often have a picture of it being all about money. Given their financial resources and the current tax law, they want to make decisions to distribute their assets at death to their heirs while minimizing taxes. Sounds simple, but what do you do when you have to divide their estate among your children, Amy the doctor, Carrie a mortgage broker, and Cindy a graphic designer? What about the family piano that has been passed down through generations? Amy, Carrie and Cindy do not play the piano, but all three children find the piano precious, not for its monetary value, but for its emotional value. While you may have left assets valued equally to each child, the two children who do not receive the family piano may think they have not been treated fairly.

What is the Emotional Value of Your Assets?

What parents do not realize is the emotional value of assets and how their children will react at the distribution of those assets. Parents should develop not only a financial balance sheet of assets, but also an emotional value sheet when determining how to distribute their estates. Parents want to treat their children fairly and, in their minds that often means equally. However, if parents take inventory of some the issues that might concern their children, they can better plan their estates for family harmony. Some of those issues include: Do we owe the children anything besides what we have already given them? How much and when should it be given or sold? What would be our conditions regarding the use of any assets we leave for our children? How should those assets with sentimental value be distributed? How do we account for differences in what we have given to our children over our lives, such as college tuition, a car, a loan, and help with medical expenses? Do our children know what we are thinking in regard to how we are distributing our assets? Should we ask the children what they want from our estate?

You Give Your Daughters Amy, Jennifer, Carrie and Cindy and Your Son Scott the Same Amount and Cindy Whines "That is Not Fair"

What is fair to one child that may not be fair to another child? Children often feel they are entitled to certain rewards and resources compared to their siblings because of their contributions to the family. For example, Cindy may be a caregiver for elder parents, while Carrie completely ignores her parents. Amy may take care of her parents' medical needs. Jennifer helps financially, but Scott cannot help because of his own special needs. If children are not treated according to what they feel they are entitled to, they will see themselves as being treated unfairly and resent parents or siblings for their "unfair" treatment. Parents have difficulty in determining what is fair. Parents often feel that all their children are entitled to the same treatment, but the problem is figuring out what is equal at a particular time. For example, her parents may have provided their daughter Amy with money to start her own business, and provided Carrie money to go to college, and helped Jennifer with funds to pay medical expenses, but those amounts of money to help Amy, Carrie and Jennifer are not the same as leaving money to Cindy or Scott twenty-five years later when mom and dad die. Often, if mom and dad leave the same amount of money to Amy, Carrie, Jennifer, Scott and Cindy, Cindy, who is receiving the money when mom and dad die, while Amy, Jennifer, Scott and Carrie received the money decades earlier, often can be expected to cry *"that's not fair."*

As Parents You Have Choices: It is OK to Treat Your Children Amy, Carrie, Jennifer, Scott and Cindy Differently and Still Be Fair

The other approach to fairness is when parents acknowledge that one child has contributed more to the family business, and therefore, children are not equally entitled to the same amount of assets. One size does not fit all. Mom and Dad can plan their estate to leave different amounts to Amy, Carrie, Jennifer, Scott and Cindy even though they love all five equally.

Despite the best efforts, sometimes sibling rivalry cannot be avoided. There are two main sources that create family conflict when parents die and their property is distributed to their children. First and foremost, children often argue over what is fair and equal. This can arise in any situation, even when parents *"leave everything equally to my children."* There are many sources of conflict caused from parent's attempt to be fair to their children. For example, when one child becomes the primary caregiver for the elderly parent, and the other child completely ignores the needs of the elderly parent, an equal division may be a cause of resentment by the child who took care of their parents.

Does Jennifer Think You are Punishing Her for Being Successful?

Another source of resentment among children is from the successful professional who has a lot more money than her brother or sister who is barely making it economically in life when her sister receives a larger portion of their parents' estate because of her *"need."* Parents often look at their children's earning capacity, education level, age, and what they have given during life to determine what percentage goes to each child. While this is a parent's choice, it can create hurt feelings and sibling rivalry. Amy the successful doctor sees the estate plan as punishment for her hard work and sacrifice in becoming successful. Amy's parents see it as simply doing what they believe is best for their children based on their children's needs at the time they made their estate plan. Before preparing the estate plan, the parents should talk to Amy, Carrie, Jennifer, Scott and Cindy. Maybe the proposed distribution is not a problem. If it is a problem, parents have a chance to explain their thinking to their children. Remember, the goal of estate planning is peace of mind, not necessarily the division of your assets.

A Salvation Army Recliner Can Be Priceless

Another source of conflict and resentment among children

is personal property. I have seen children spend more money fighting over a valueless recliner and incurring hurt feelings that get in the way of logic. I recall the situation where grandpa left his shot gun to his then longtime girlfriend and his grandson spent good money in court litigating over the validity of the Will, because he knew his grandfather would have wanted to leave the shot gun to him. More money was spent on litigation, than what the shot gun was worth.

When making your estate plan, you should be given the option to prepare personal property memorandum regarding tangible personal property that has intrinsic value. For example, sentimental items, reminders, photos, jewelry, artwork and collectibles are often the subject of bitter disputes as to how they should be divided among heirs. This is a very easy problem to solve simply by preparing a personal property memorandum to be included with your estate planning documents so that you may properly divide these items yourself. Once you have made the property division, communicate openly with your children as to why and how you made the decision. This heads off the emotional conflict that can lead to a property fight after you have died.

Hard Work, Low Pay, Lack of Appreciation -- The Reward for Your Trustee

Trust administration is not an honorary position. Many important decisions are made by the administrator of your estate or the trustee and require a serious commitment of time. For example, if you leave your estate through a trust, the trustee must invest and administer trust assets pursuant to stringent fiduciary laws in order to determine the propriety of distributions to trust beneficiaries, maintain accurate records of accounts, make allocations between income and principal, and see that all tax returns are filed. Clients who come in the office often want the oldest son or daughter to be the either the Executor and/or successor trustee to manage the administration of their estates. While the oldest child may be the most competent to perform the duties described above, the other children that are excluded from power may be jealous if they were not named as the administrator or trustee, and may challenge every decision made by their brother or sister, thus lining the pockets of lawyers and experts, incurring the costs and expenses that you attempted to avoid by planning your estate before your death.

Co-Trustees, Conflict Solver or Conflict Creator?

To avoid potential conflict, you have two choices regarding trustees depending upon the size of your estate. First, a professional trustee can be appointed as the successor trustee, who would act independently to manage the trust or estate for the benefit of the beneficiaries. In the alternative, under the rules of the Oregon Uniform Trust Code, Co-trustees can be named to manage your trust assets. The Trust Code provides methods for Co-trustees to reach decisions and establishes what exposure to liability trustees have in administering trusts. While this does not solve the problem, having all the children as Co-trustees increases the likelihood of eliminating conflict. The extent to which any of your children do not want to act as Co-trustees, under the Oregon Trust Code, they can disclaim the position. Having been given the chance to serve as trustee and understanding the duties of the trustee, the child that disclaims may want to cooperate with the child who is acting as a trustee or Executor.

While it is generally a good arrangement to have multiple Co- trustees serving together, such an arrangement will not work well if there is already animosity between the children, or if the children have different economic goals.

Mom Needs Money Now: The Children Want Assets Later When Mom Dies

Another source of conflict is when parents have set up a trust for their assets that is effective upon the death of the first spouse, but before the second spouse dies. For example, a tax planning technique often used to minimize or eliminate federal estate tax is to place a portion of the deceased spouse's assets into a Credit Shelter Trust. Generally a Credit Shelter Trust is set up to provide the surviving spouse with an income from the Trust during her life and any assets remaining at the spouse's death will pass to the children. The wife can also receive distributions of principal from the Trust at the trustee's discretion during her lifetime. Either because of the size of the estate or to save money, one of the children is named as the trustee of the Credit Shelter

Trust. This can cause friction because the surviving spouse may need a portion of the principal to live on and is forced to ask her child for money which came from her and her husband in the first place. A second concern is that when the surviving spouse dies, the remainder in the Trust will pass to the children. However, during the surviving spouse's lifetime, the income from the Trust goes to the support of the surviving spouse. This creates conflict and tension because the children want the Trust assets to be as large as possible when mom dies, while the surviving spouse wants the assets in Trust invested in income producing assets that will support her during his or her lifetime.

Yours, Mine and Ours

An inherent conflict occurs when there are children are from a blended family. When you are in a second marriage and you have children from one spouse's prior marriage and the current marriage, or from both the husband and wife's prior marriages, using the various planning tools to prevent family conflict is essential. Ideally, before entering into a second marriage, you have a Prenuptial Agreement. However, if you do not have a Prenuptial Agreement, decisions will have to made as to how to handle assets when the husband dies and whether or not he is willing to give his current wife the power to determine how to leave the family estate when she dies. If you are in a second marriage and have children with your previous spouse, you must make provisions for your children and do not assume that your new spouse will take care of your children. If you do what many clients want to do, *"leave everything to my second spouse,"* there is nothing to force your second spouse to leave everything to your children.

The Loan to Amy

One of the greatest sources of conflict when you die is that *"loan"* to one of your children. We have all been in the position to wanting to have our children get ahead when they are financially short. For example, lending your daughter Amy money for a down payment on her first home, loaning Carrie money for her college education, lending Cindy money to help with her medical expenses, lending money to Scott for transportation, and lending money to Jennifer for family help, helping all your children get braces for your grandchildren, and lending Carrie money when she was unemployed are actions that many parents take on behalf of their children. This is part of being a parent; however, some of the most horrific litigation occurs over the loan to the child that was never repaid. The usual scenario is that the child, say Amy, who received the money will claim that mom or dad forgave the loan and, therefore, there was no intent that it be taken out of her share as debt at the time of her parents' death. Carrie, Jennifer, Scott and Cindy see it differently. They see that Amy, who received the loan, owes it to their parents' estate. Carrie, Jennifer, Scott and Cindy believe they are entitled to a share of that money. In addition, not only do Carrie, Jennifer, Scott and Cindy feel entitled to a share of the money, but they feel entitled to a share of the interest that money would have earned if it had been repaid shortly after the time it was loaned to the Amy twenty-five years ago. This is personal. Children will spend more money in litigation costs over a relatively small loan than any person not emotionally involved would incur.

Can You Prevent Conflict Among Your Children And Preserve Harmony After You Are Gone? Maybe or Maybe Not

One method often used in Wills or Trusts is a *"No Contest Clause"* which provides that if one of your children who is entitled to receive a share of your assets challenges the validity of the Will or the Trust, then he or she receives nothing. While this is no guarantee that your children will not file a lawsuit over the administration of your assets after you die, it does provide a financial incentive for your children to work together with the administration of your assets.

Fair, equal, and family harmony are meritorious goals for any estate plan. No matter how you involve your children, the ultimate decision of who gets what, falls on the parents' shoulders. Parents have to decide for themselves what they owe their children. They have to decide if equal is fair. It is your decision of what is fair and not what your children think is fair that matters. After thinking about it, you may decide that the only thing you can give equally to your children is your love.

CHAPTER 11

PROTECTING YOUR CHILD'S INHERITANCE FROM CREDITORS, PREDATORS, EX-SPOUSES AND AFLUENZA

If you ask most people what estate planning is, the most frequent answer would be, *"leaving my property to my spouse and children."* There is a misconception among many people that estate planning is only for the wealthy and ignore the reality that with the proper estate planning, you can plan for situations like disability, incapacity while you are alive, leave your property to your beneficiaries while minimizing federal and state taxes, providing for the care of children should you die before they reach the age of majority, avoid Probate, and reduce taxes. Though the goal of most individuals is to leave an inheritance to their spouse or children, leaving an outright inheritance to either your spouse or children overlooks the fact that your estate that you have worked hard all your life to create may not go to the benefit of those you intend to take care of later in life. For example, money that you may leave to your children can be lost through divorce, through poor financial management, through lawsuits, be subject to investment scams, or simply lost due to reckless spending.

Whether the risk is losing your child's inheritance to his or her creditors, whether your children have a risk of blowing their inheritance either because of poor money management, addiction, financial immaturity, or to a soon to be ex-spouse who receives a large portion of your child's inheritance when the divorce is final, or from affluenza, also known as spending large sums of money within a very short period of time, there are estate planning techniques that will enhance the likelihood that your intention to leave certain assets to certain people will be carried out and these same assets shielded from these predators.

Contract from Beyond

Through the simple devise of establishing a revocable living trust which upon your death creates two separate irrevocable trusts, a Credit Shelter Trust and an unlimited Marital Deduction Trust, the later properly established as a QTIP trust, ensures that you direct who eventually receives your estate upon the death of your spouse, while providing lifetime income to your spouse. You can control from the grave where your estate will go upon your spouse's death and avoid having your surviving spouse share your estate with her new husband, or leave your estate to someone other than your children at the time of her death.

Use Exempt Properties for Protection

Estate planners have a large toolbox of tools, strategies and techniques that can be used individually or in combination to protect your assets from the bad guys, such as creditors, collectors and scam artist while you are living, and to protect your beneficiary's inheritance after you die. With respect to creditors, state law and federal bankruptcy law provides certain exemptions for property which the exempt from attachment by creditors.

Balancing Equity with the Homestead and Bank Deposit Exemptions

Two major exemptions that can be used in all estate plans are the homestead exemption and the bank deposit exemption. In Washington the homestead exemption is $125,000, while in Oregon it is a paltry $40,000. While it is always a challenge to determine how the value of your home will trend, a high risk individual, an attorney or doctor, might want to maintain equity in his or her home that approaches the homestead exemption. This will provide a level of safety. While the same funds could earn a return in a mutual fund, unless the fund was a qualified retirement plan, it would offer no wealth protection to the high risk individual. This is also true for a very limited amount of bank accounts.

The Qualified Retirement Account Exemption- Win Win for Accumulation and Preservation

The third exemption of importance is the exemption for qualified ERISA retirement accounts, IRAs, and pensions. A very simple strategy is to maximize the amount you put in your "qualified" tax-deferred retirement plans such as your pension, IRA, and 401(k). Not only does this strategy provide wealth protection, but it provides for tax deferment, growth of funds, and has little downside as long as you keep you funds in the plan until 59 1/2, [but it provides for tax deferment, growth of funds, and has no withdrawal penalty after 59 ½.Most states, including Washington and Oregon protect 100% of the assets in such accounts.

Other Exemptions That Can Protect Assets

Further states protect a limited dollar amount of bank deposits, building materials, cemetery and burial plots, personal bodily injury claims, fraternal benefits, health and medical savings accounts, annuity payments, motor vehicles, personal property, public assistance, veteran's benefits, tools of the trade, wages, and workers compensation. While these exemptions are limited in dollar amount and are not available in all states, full advantage should be taken of these exemptions if asset protection before any claims occur is an issue for you.

While exemption planning provides some protection, clearly not all assets can be held in exempt form. Exemptions, just like any other wealth preservation tools, require implementation before there are storm clouds on the horizon. You must take action now. Waiting can cause loss of your assets that could be prevented. If there current judgments or creditors, or reasonably foreseeable claims, wealth preservation strategies will not work. Further, under the current bankruptcy law there are limitations on exemption planning.

Why Adding Children to Title is a Bad Idea and Gifting Doesn't Work

People sometimes believe that if they give their assets to their spouse or children, they can avoid exposure to lawsuits and creditors. Gifting usually does not work whether it is to a spouse or to children. Gifting to children can trigger a gift tax and may be treated as a fraudulent conveyance for purposes of hindering a creditor. In addition, to the extent you retain joint control with your child, such as putting your child on the title to your home, you subject your property to lawsuits filed against your child.

Similar problems arise if you attempt to gift to a spouse. There is no gift tax issue. However, any assets given to a spouse are still subject to lawsuits filed against the spouse. Further, depending on state law, the gift may be excluded from the definition of marital property, and in the case of divorce, the spouse may receive all of the property gifted as well as 50% of the marital property. Another problem with gifting is that most states, including Oregon, have a fraudulent conveyance law, which for a certain period of time, will undo any transfers when there is a present creditor and the joint owners are unable to meet debts.

The use of joint tenants or joint ownership is only effective with respect to the death of one spouse. A joint tenancy in Oregon provides some protection for a couple's residence, but does not provide protection for joint deaths. If both spouses are liable on a debt or for taxes due, to the extent the property is not exempt, the creditor would proceed against the joint tenancy property. With respect to federal tax claims, the IRS can claim against and attach joint property even though its tax claim is against only one spouse.

Insurance to Pay Judgments and Defend Lawsuits

We live in society where the solution for every little wrong is to sue someone. There does not have to be any merit in a claim to file a lawsuit. Once a lawsuit is filed, regardless of merit, everyone loses. You can win a lawsuit by successfully defending and still lose because of the loss of time, emotion and costs. You are at risk of being the victim of a frivolous lawsuit. You could lose your business if you are not protected. You may win a lawsuit, but you could still lose the battle.

Defending a lawsuit, even if you are victorious, will cost you as much as $50,000.

Do frivolous lawsuits occur? The following are real lawsuits:

- A fan successfully sued San Diego and Jack Murphy Stadium for $5.4 million over failure to be able to pee. The fan was at an Elton John concert and in his complaint alleged he was caused embarrassment and emotional distress when he tried to use the restrooms and all of them had women using a urinal. Thanks to the sight of a women using a urinal in front of him. The basis of his lawsuit was that he was too embarrassed to share the public bathrooms with women.

- Another man sued a the public library for $1.5 million because his 50-pound Labrador was attacked by the library's 12-pound feline mascot;

- A high school basketball player was awarded $1.5 million by a jury for an eating disorder caused after her basketball coach yelled at her to lose 10 pounds, eat nutritiously, and stay away from junk food. A jury of her peers decided that this action caused the player's eating disorder;

- A women broke her ankle when she tripped over her own toddler. The toddler was running through the store unsupervised when mom tripped over her. The jury entered a $780,000 judgment against the store;

- A man sued a nudie bar claiming whiplash and mental anguish. The cause of his whiplash? H received a lap dance, and the dancer's breast where so large that when they hit him during the dance it caused his injury. The jury denied after trial his claim for $15,000; and

- A man was trying to steal his neighbor's hub caps. One problem, his neighbor was in the car. The neighbor started the car and ran over the soon to be bandits hand. The jury awarded medical expenses plus $74,000 to the would be bandit.

The first line of defense is to purchase liability insurance. Liability insurance will usually cover tort liability. However, insurance companies protect themselves and add exclusions to their policies that exclude coverage for a claim. Another problem with insurance policies is that they are for a specific amount and the amount of the claim may exceed the amount of the insurance policy limit, a condition known as "over policy limit claim." Finally, you may be able to purchase insurance for a specific risk that you feel might occur in the future.

Marriage Has Become a Business Agreement

Another method of protecting specific assets is through a Pre- Marital Agreement. A Pre-Marital agreement provides that certain assets belong to each spouse at the time of marriage and as long as the assets are not co-mingled, would remain the assets of the spouse that brought them to the marriage upon divorce. Pre-Marital agreements can be effective as to specific assets, but present a practical problem in negotiating an agreement with your soon-to-be spouse and in handling the assets in such a manner to preserve their status as separate property. If you do not want to dim the feel of love by negotiating with your future spouse, consider a Pre-Nuptial Trust. The safest method is to use both a Pre-Marital Agreement and Pre-Marital Trust.

Business Structures Can Provide Some Protection

For family owned businesses or high worth professionals, methods of asset protection, combined with a family limited partnership or a limited liability company, are used for an additional layer of protection. However, creditors can attack the limited partnership interest where partnership interests are subject to fraudulent conveyance statutes, or through a creditor obtaining a judgment and stepping into the shoes of the debtor and potentially judicially foreclosing on a partnership interest. First, a debtor cannot transfer individual assets to a limited partner or limited liability company when there is a pending claim unless they provide for the existing claims. Such a transaction would constitute a fraudulent conveyance and would provide no protection. However, in Oregon and some other states, a debtor can obtain a charging order against the debtor's share of the limited liability company and obtain the rights of assignee of the membership interest. If the charging order is against a limited liability company, in Oregon, the charging order constitutes a lien on the debtor's transferable interest and a court may order foreclosure of the interest subject to the charging order. The purchaser at a foreclosure sale would have the rights of a transferee and their interest could be redeemed by having the debt paid off. Further, to the extent that the debtor files for bankruptcy, courts which have addressed the issue have disregarded any charging order protection and foreclosed directly on the interest of the debtor in the limited liability company.

A-B Trust Planning Can Protect Beneficiaries

While the above entities can be very powerful planning tools, they will not serve their purpose if they are not funded properly, maintained annually, and all formalities of the business are followed. If a parent is the general partner, a limited partnership will not provide asset protection for the parents' assets.

The most common estate planning technique for reasonably significant sized estates is the A-B trust plan also known as the marital trust or bypass trust. The A trust is a trust that provides for the unlimited marital deduction and usually includes a QTIP, power of appointment, or a spousal remainder trust. The B trust is a Credit Shelter Trust or exemption trust that provides for exclusion of federal estate taxes and deferral of Oregon inheritance taxes up to the respective exemption amounts. To protect beneficiaries from either their own foolishness or from creditors, these trusts will usually contain a spend thrift provision which prevents a beneficiary from pledging or otherwise alienating his beneficial interest, unless the settlor is also a beneficiary. A spend thrift will generally prevent creditors from attaching to a beneficiary interest. Oregon is in the minority of states that has adopted the Uniform Trust Code which has a specific provision recognizing the spend thrift trust provision.

Oregon Abolishes Discretionary Support Trust and Probably Eliminates the Protection of Spendthrift Trust

Prior to the adoption of the Uniform Trust Code in Oregon, asset protection was also provided by discretionary trust. A discretionary trust provides that distributions from the trust to the beneficiaries will be made in the sole and absolute discretion of the trustee. Prior to the enactment of the Uniform Trust Code ("UTC") in Oregon there were two primary types of asset protection under common law. The discretionary trust and the spendthrift provision. Discretionary trusts are based upon the discretion of the trustee to make distributions in his sole discretion. The beneficiary does not have an enforceable right to a distribution. Absent a right to enforce a distribution, the beneficiary's interest is not a property interest, but is a mere expectancy. A creditor cannot reach an interest that is a mere expectancy. Similarly the spendthrift provision protects beneficiaries from having creditors attach the assets of the trust and forcing a distribution to the beneficiary in satisfaction of the creditor's claim.

In Oregon, absent a spendthrift provision, the UTC appears to allow any creditor to attach present or future distributions from any trust, including a discretionary trust. This contradicts the majority of prior law.

Go Shopping – You May Need a Trust Outside Home State

Sometimes it may be advantageous to move assets to another State to take advantage of their laws. For example, under existing Oregon law it is not clear whether the beneficiary protection from creditors sought by the decedent can be accomplished. A trust can be established in a state that has more favorable laws with respect to recognition of the long history of the discretionary distribution interest and provides that a discretionary interest is neither an enforceable right nor a property interest. If protection of a beneficiary's inheritance is an important goal in your estate plan, then consideration should be given to establishing a trust outside of Oregon in one of the states with favorable laws

CHAPTER 12

STRETCHING IS GOOD--AVOID REDUCING YOUR RETIREMENT BENEFITS THROUGH THIS STRATEGY AND BE LOVED FOR GENERATIONS

Don't Outlive Your IRA, Have Your IRA Outlive You, Your Spouse and Your Children

What assets do most people have when they die? Most of the people who come to me for estate planning, especially if they have made it into the fifties or sixties will have three major assets that make up most of their wealth. What are those assets you ask? Usually those three assets will be a life insurance policy, a home that is paid for, and some form of retirement account usually a 401K, 403B or IRA account. This makes retirement accounts one of the most important assets to plan for in your estate plan.

When you create your estate plan you have to give special consideration to your retirement plans because:

- They will unusually be one of, if not your largest asset;
- A retirement plan does not pass by your Last Will and Testament;
- A retirement plan does not pass by a Revocable Living Trust;
- A retirement plan can provide one of the greatest tax breaks that you can pass down to the next generation;
- You can control from the grave how this money is saved, grown or spent; and
- You can avoid the cost, time, and public display of Probate.

One of the biggest mistakes that people make is not preserving the tax deferral benefits of their qualified retirement plans. Most of the mistakes come from ignorance and lack of planning. People do not realize that their retirement plan money can be taxed immediately on death or the tax can be deferred over decades. Think about it, would you rather pay a large tax now or over five years, or have it grow tax deferred it over the lifetime of your children? Almost 100% of the time prospective clients want it to grow for decades tax deferred.

To see the benefits of maintaining your funds in a tax deferred plan, assume that you leave $100,000 in a qualified retirement plan in trust for Scott, your 40-year-old child. If Scott withdraws and spends the money from the retirement plan both the principal and interest withdrawn is taxed as income tax. In a very short time the money will be gone.

On the other hand, if the money is retained in the an inherited IRA by Scott, and it is left in the IRA until Scott reaches age 60, growing tax deferred at 6% per year will result in Scott having $264,58 in the account. Scott can take the funds out based on his life expectancy, which will allow him to keep the account growing tax deferred until he is 70 ½ when he will start to with draw the funds based on then life expectancy.

What are the Types of Retirement Plans We are Talking About When We Consider How to Save Taxes Over Multiple Generations?

There are three basic types of retirement plans:

- Traditional IRA
- 401K and 403 B; and
- Roth IRAs, 401K and 403B.

A **Traditional IRA** means an Individual Retirement Account that you set up for savings. You put money in with after tax dollars and then when you file your tax return you receive a deduction on your income for the amount you have contributed for the year. There are limits on the amount that you can contribute each year. In 2017 for a Roth or Traditional IRA contribution is limited to $ 5,500 if you are under 50 and $6,500 if you are over 50. 401K and 403 b limits are $ 18,000 and

$ 24,000 if you are over 50.

The characteristics of an **IRA** are:

- You cannot be covered by your employer's retirement plan;
- There is a certain dollar limit each year;
- When you withdraw the money it is subject to income tax;
- Withdrawals prior to 59 ½ are subject to a penalty, but after that you can withdraw without penalty; and
- You must begin to take a percentage of your money out when you are 70 ½.

401K Plans are employer sponsored and investment choices are based on the plan administrator's selection. You usually have a choice of several investment options, but the investments are not unlimited. The basic features of a 401K are:

- You invest pretax dollars;
- The money is taken directly out of your paycheck;
- Your employer can match your contributions if it so elects;
- You taxable income is reduced by the amount of your personal contribution;
- The money in your account grows tax deferred;
- If you withdraw prior to 59 ½ you will pay a 10% penalty;
- You must start taking withdrawals at age 70 ½ based on your life expectancy; and
- Your withdrawals are subject to income tax.

403 B plans are like **401K** plans except they are for school employees and nonprofit organizations.

The third type of retirement plan is a **Roth IRA (**and in some cases a Roth 401K or Roth 403B). These plans provide:

- They are funded with after tax dollars;
- You do not receive a tax deduction when you make the contribution;
- The earnings are tax free;
- There is no mandatory withdrawal age;
- Withdrawals are tax free; and
- There are certain limits on the amount of contributions and the earned income limits for individuals and couples.

You Can Lose 70% of Your Retirement Plan by Failing to Plan

The importance of planning for qualified plans and IRAs is increasing because the value of these plans and the percentage of a couple's estate it comprises has grown significantly over the years since employers starting providing these plans as an employee benefit. Further, until recently with the recession, a significant number of employers provided a match up to as high as 6% which encouraged employees to contribute to receive the matching contribution.

I have seen over the years retirements account lost, and lost quickly, due to heavy taxes and quick spend downs, through the failure to have a proper plan in place. Further, this inherited plan assets withdrawn over a relatively short period of time can become lost not only through income and estate taxes, but by claims by a beneficiary's judgment creditors, to spouses of your beneficiaries through divorce, through financial irresponsibility by beneficiaries, spending the money rather than saving it for their retirement, and financial mismanagement of the money.

How your assets are distributed upon your death depends on how old you are and who is going to receive your account. Assume that your spouse predeceased you and your children are your beneficiaries.

If you die before you are 70 ½ your children will have to start withdrawing funds the year after your death, but it will be based on their life expectancies; and if you die after you are 70 ½ your children take the amount you would have taken in the year that your died, then the amount is calculated based on your children's life expectancy.

Roth IRA and Roth 401K

Who inherits your account determines when the money has to be withdrawn. Remember while you were alive, because you paid into your Roth account with after tax dollars, you did not have to start any withdrawal. However, when you die, no matter who inherits it, your spouse or your children, they have to withdraw funds, but can in some cases continue to be tax deferred on earned income.

If you spouse inherits the account, he or she can roll the money over into their own Roth IRA and continue to keep the money in the rolled over Roth IRA; and if your children inherit the Roth IRA or Roth 401K the distribution rules for a regular IRA or 401K apply and they will have to start taking money out the year after the decedent's death based on their expected lifetime. The funds grow tax free and no tax is paid on withdrawal.

Here is how a Roth IRA might work for your children. You are full retirement age but you keep working. Because you keep working after full retirement age, you can draw your social security check without penalty, but you do not need your social security to live on. Instead, you put your social security check in a Roth IRA for 10 years until you decide to retire. When you do retire you live off your social security and your 401K taxable required minimum withdrawals. You die ten years later, so the money in the Roth IRA has now grown over a 20 year period. You leave you Roth IRA to Kathy, your wife, who is the designated beneficiary. Kathy outlives you by another 10 years, 30 years since you opened the account. Kathy has named your daughter Cindy as the beneficiary. Cindy is 45 when she inherits the Roth IRA and she must take out the funds over her life expectancy. Because of her age very little has to be withdrawn each year. Not only does she receive the money the rest of her life, but it is tax free. Cindy will thank you for contributing to a Roth IRA for 10 years and have it provide income for decades thereafter.

Do It Right and Your Spouse and Children Will Thank You

The timing of the required distributions after death depends on the type of plan, who the beneficiary is, and when you die. This is a complicated area of the law and one that should be planned for with the help of an experienced retirement plan attorney. As we have seen, money can be withdrawn quickly or slowly. Only Designated Beneficiaries get to withdraw Traditional IRA and 401K money slowly. So who are these lucky Designated Beneficiaries? Two of the lucky winners as Designated Beneficiaries are your spouse and your children.

The easiest method if you are married is to name your husband or wife. Not only are they Designated Beneficiaries, but husbands and wives get special treatment from the IRS.

Two of the most used strategies are:

- Wait to withdraw money from a Traditional IRA or 401k until the spouse reaches age 70 ½ ; and

- The surviving spouse can name a new beneficiary with a continuing tax deferral benefit.

In addition, the surviving wife or husband can keep the plan in the name of the deceased person. Why would the surviving wife or husband want to do this you may be asking? First, the survivor can wait to start taking distributions until her deceased spouse would have been 70 ½, but take the RMD based on his or her own life expectancy. This benefits the survivor when he or she is older than the deceased spouse. Second, if the survivor needs to withdraw the funds, there is no penalty.

Another option for the survivor is to roll over the account to his or her own Traditional Rollover IRA. With this option, the survivor can wait to withdraw funds until he or she reaches 70 ½. Further, the survivor can name a child or someone else as a beneficiary of the Rollover IRA. The child can then use a stretch out time period to defer taxes on the growth of the fund over their lifetime.

Can You Plan Around Your Spouse?

A spouse has a right in your Retirement Plan. A spouse can only waive that right in writing. Otherwise he or she will be the primary beneficiary on you Retirement Plan. If you don't name your spouse as the primary beneficiary he or she will have a right to have of the funds in a community property state and under federal law a spouse without waiver is entitled to all the Retirement Account.

What Happens if You are the Surviving Spouse or You and Your Spouse Agree to Name the Children as Beneficiaries of Your Traditional IRA or 401K Account?

If you children are really children, under 18 in most states, they cannot own assets or inherit directly. If you leave your account on your beneficiary form to your children, the court will appoint a Guardian and Conservator for them until they reach 18. At 18 they get the money. Will they leave the money in the account and defer taxes over their lifetime or will they spend it as most 18 year olds would do?   I would bet that they will spend it on something frivolous and owe a ton of taxes on the withdrawals.

How about leaving it in **Trust** or in a **Uniform Gift to Minor Act** account. This will at least provide some management of the funds until 21. Further, under the Trust option, the funds could be managed until a time you designated in the trust and distributions made under the RMD will be based on the oldest child's lifetime. Check your plan's rules, some of them require a full payout in five years. That is why you get a copy of your plan when you do your estate planning.

I Have Five Children, They are All Adults, Can't I Just Leave it to All of Them Equally?

We always want to be fair and equal. With most assets we can divide it equally. With a Traditional IRA or 401K that is not a good idea. Assume that your children are 45, 40, 30, 25, and 20. If you designate them as beneficiaries equally, each will receive 1/5 of the account. However, they have to split the account by September 30th of the year of the parent's death. What if they fail to make that change by the deadline? Then the age of the oldest child, 45 in this case, is used to determine the life expectancy of all five children and the length of time over which this taxable money has to be withdrawn. For the twenty five year old child, he or she lost 20 years of tax deferral growth.

IRA Stand Alone Trust and the Stretch-Out

One estate planning device that is used to address special situations is an IRA standalone trust. The IRA stand-alone trust is particularly appropriate when beneficiaries may be financially irresponsible, have special medical needs, have developmental disabilities, may be in marriages that could result in divorce, or are in a high risk professional profession. The IRA stand-alone trust is also beneficial if the deceased wants to control distributions after his death and to compel long-term tax deferral of the investment.

In order for beneficiaries of an IRA trust to be treated as designated beneficiaries of the IRA trust, they must meet the following requirement s: (1) the trust must be valid under state law; (2) the trust is irrevocable or becomes irrevocable at the participant's death; (3) the trust contains identifiable beneficiaries; and (4) a copy is provided to the plan administrator on or before October 31 in the year after the participant's death.

The plan documents control whether or not distributions from the plan assets can be stretched out over an extended period of time. Utilizing the separate stand-alone retirement trust, the trust can be set up as a conduit trust which passes the RMD directly to the primary beneficiary or as an accumulation trust is where the trustee decides when the distribution is made. These trusts can also be designed so that they toggle between a conduit and an accumulation trust to provide a control over the beneficiary's use of the funds.

In order for beneficiaries of an IRA trust to be treated as designated beneficiaries of the IRA trust, they must meet the following requirement s: (1) the trust must be valid under state law; (2) the trust is irrevocable or becomes irrevocable at the participant's death; (3) the trust contains identifiable beneficiaries; and (4) a copy is provided to the plan administrator on or before October 31 in the year after the participant's death.

The plan documents control whether or not distributions from the plan assets can be stretched out over an extended period of time. Utilizing the separate stand-alone retirement trust, the trust can be set up as a conduit trust which passes the RMD directly to the primary beneficiary or as an accumulation trust is where the trustee decides when the distribution is made. These trusts can also be designed so that they toggle between a conduit and an accumulation trust to provide a control over the beneficiary's use of the funds.

Benefits of the IRA Stand Alone Trust

Why not just name the beneficiaries of your retirement plan outright, instead of using a trust? Using a trust provides more assurance that you will see your goals are achieved and provides the maximum stretch out of distributions with the accumulation of returns and tax deferral. Depending on state law, the trust may provide more asset protection against creditors and upon divorce of one of the beneficiaries. In addition, the assets can be kept under the current advisor's management.

When Not to Use an IRA Stand Alone Trust

There are costs involved in annual maintenance expenses in maintaining an IRA stand-alone trust. Therefore, most planners recommend that an IRA trust not be considered until an IRA or qualified plan has approximately $200,000 of assets. There are other plans, strategies, and techniques that can be used with an IRA depending on the size of your estate.

CHAPTER 13

DON'T MAKE UNCLE SAM THE BENEFICIARY OF YOUR LIFE INSURANCE

Death -- One of the Certain to Happen Events

Life insurance is a unique animal. Life insurance is better than a sure thing. You bet that you will die and the only question is when. Accordingly, life insurance can create an estate with monthly payments. If set up properly, life insurance has tax advantages, and it can provide liquidity for many different needs at the time of death.

Life insurance can provide funds to pay off the mortgage at death, pay death taxes and pay estate costs.

The liquidity provided from life insurance can avoid at the time of death the fire sale of assets to pay taxes and estate costs, provide funds for your children's college education, provide liquidity to repay loans and other debts owed by decedent, provide for the orderly transfer of business interest at death, and help equalize inheritances when some children have a business interest and other children are not interested in maintaining the family business.

Life Insurance is Not Tax Free but It Can Be

One misconception about life insurance is that it is tax free. Although the general rule is that life insurance proceeds are income tax free to the beneficiary, life insurance proceeds may be subject to federal estate tax, state inheritance tax, gift tax and generation skipping tax. The general rule is that life insurance proceeds are subject to estate tax if the decedent's estate exceeds the exemption amount and if the policy holder has *incidents of ownership,* or the proceeds are payable to the *estate. Incidents of ownership* include the policy holder's right to change beneficiaries, to borrow the cash value, to select dividend options, or change premium payment schedules. Even with respect to income tax, when distributions during life are made from permanent life insurance from the cash surrender value, the amount of money received above the basis in the policy can be taxable income depending on other factors.

Options to Make Life Insurance Proceeds Non-Taxable

There are several options for avoiding ownership of the policy and inclusion in your estate when you die. You can give the policy to another person or you can create an **Irrevocable Life Insurance Trust ("ILIT")** and transfer ownership to the ILIT. A life insurance policy is considered a gift when transferred after the initial purchase. The value of the gift is the interpolated terminal reserve in the policy at the time of transfer. This amount will be provided by the life insurance company on request. There may be federal gift tax consequences if the amount exceeds the annual exclusion, which in 2017 is $14,000. However, if your total estate is less than $5.49 million, it can be part of your lifetime exclusion amount. While there is no gift tax in Oregon, you may want to remove the life insurance policy from your estate because Oregon has a much lower taxable threshold. To transfer your life insurance policy, you must do it with forms approved by your insurer to make the transfer is effective.

The Three Year Claw Back Rule

Whether the transfer is made to another person or to an ILIT, if you are transferring an existing policy and you die within 3 years of the date of the transfer the policy, the policy proceeds are pulled back into your estate for federal estate tax purposes and for Oregon tax purposes as if you had remained owner of the policy.

Designation of Beneficiaries

A Will controls the disposition of life insurance proceeds only if the estate is the designated beneficiary. Otherwise, the beneficiary designation in the policy will control. The beneficiary designation in the policy should be consistent with your will or trust and meet your estate planning goals.

Give Up Control to Save Taxes

To make a transfer and take the life insurance proceeds out of your estate, you must give up control and not retain any *"incidents of ownership"*. Changing or naming beneficiaries, borrowing against the policy, surrendering, converting or canceling the policy, paying premiums or selecting payment options are all considered *"incidents of ownership"* which will draw the policy proceeds back into your estate when you die. While life insurance policies, if set up correctly, can be an excellent way to pass assets tax free to your beneficiaries, to avoid having the proceeds included in your estate, you must give up control. For example, give up *"incidents of ownership"* using an ILIT. Once the ILIT is established and funded the terms of the ILIT cannot be changed. Further, you cannot be the trustee of the ILIT or the person who controls the policy.

Creating an ILIT requires following strict rules and forces

you to maintain a system to pay the premiums annually while avoiding gift taxes. Once you have established an ILIT, the trustee of the ILIT will be the owner of the policy and the beneficiary will be the ILIT. The transfer of ownership is irrevocable and you will not be able to borrow on the existing life insurance policy or else it will be considered a part of your taxable estate upon your death. Funds will have to be transferred into an ILIT bank account run by the trustee with a tax payer identification number for the ILIT to pay the initial premium for the purchase of the life insurance policy and to fund the annual premium payment each year with further gifts. The transfer of funds to an ILIT may trigger a gift tax and require you to use a portion of your lifetime gift exclusion. If the amount needed to pay the annual premium is significant, then the ILIT may be set up as a Crummy Trust where you gift money to the trust for the benefit of the beneficiaries, which are usually your children or spouse, with the idea that the beneficiaries will benefit from the proceeds at your death. However, in order to make the gifts non-taxable when you gift money to the ILIT, notice has to be provided to the beneficiaries and the beneficiaries allowed a reasonable time, usually 30 days, to take the gift out of the trust or let the right to remove the gift lapse and the trustee can then pay the life insurance premiums.

When you set up an ILIT, the beneficiary is the trust. As part of your trust document, the trustee should be required to first pay estate taxes due, state inheritance taxes due, and any other expenses out of the proceeds. To the extent that there are funds remaining after expenses are paid, those will be distributed to the beneficiaries of the trust according to the terms of the trust instrument.

This chapter has only addressed some of the issues which can be resolved using life insurance to attack the stain of income, estate and gift taxes. Only an estate planning professional can help you determine the appropriate type of insurance for your particular needs and which planning techniques are appropriate for your situation. As with planning for retirement benefits, insurance planning requires close cooperation between your financial consultant and your estate planning attorney.

CHAPTER 14

MAN'S BEST FRIEND – PROVIDING FOR DAISY AND DUCHESS

Planning for Your Pet In Case He or She Outlives You- What Would Happen to Daisy and Duchess if You Didn't Come Home?

What would happen to Daisy and Duchess, my two dogs, if I didn't come home? Every night when I come home from work, my two dogs bark when the car enters the driveway, give me the eagle eye as I get my brief case out of the car and start the walk to the door, set at the glass door and wag their tails, get excited and can't wait for me to open the door, drop my brief case and give them the love and attention they deserve. Sound familiar? For many pet owners, they repeat this ritual day after day. Some pet owners are lucky enough they don't even have to leave their pets during the day.

Does this ever happen at your house? We have quite a routine from the loving greeting, to a bout of play, to relaxing together in my recliner, to preparation for bed where they sleep with me, to getting their treats before they retire for the night. Yes, my pets are family. They are like another of my children. Americans are a pet-loving nation.

I have had dogs all my life. My first dog at the tender age of 3 was a Collie. At that time there was a famous TV dog, Lassie, so my Collie was named Lassie. I outlived Lassie and went through a period of sadness, tears, and depression when Lassie passed away. This pattern has been repeated many times over my life since dogs have a shorter life span than humans.

Now that I am a Baby Boomer, for the first time I realized that Daisy and Duchess might outlive me. I ignored over the years the fact that an unexpected automobile accident, a fall down a flight of stairs, or a natural disaster like an earthquake, flood or hurricane could take me from Daisy and Duchess and leave them helpless and lost. What would happen to your cat or dog if you and your wife or husband did not come home one day?

If You Do Not Plan, Your Pet May Have an Uncertain Future

Can your cat or dog take care of themselves if you did not come home today? In my case, what would happen to Daisy and

Duchess if I could not take care of their needs? You have your own Daisy and Duchess and they deserve your thoughtful planning while you are alive. You probably have a sister or brother, or son or daughter who has told you they would care for Daisy and Duchess when you are gone. However, your brother or sister has not really thought of what it costs and the time commitment to take care of Daisy and Duchess.

The cost of properly caring for Daisy and Duchess can be significant. Just think of the cost of food, medicine, grooming, trips to the vets, and kennel cost when the family takes a vacation. It can add up really fast. While you were willing to incur those expenses, will your son or daughter be willing to incur those expenses for the long haul? And what about the time commitment for walks, play time, brushing, giving vitamins, putting out fresh water, feeding, and loving Daisy and Duchess. Will they take on the commitment you have given Daisy and Duchess. If not, Daisy and Duchess could go from sitting on your lap to being alone and frightened at the local shelter.

If you do not plan ahead, your pet may have an uncertain future. You can take care of one of the problems-the cost of caring for Daisy and Duchess-through setting aside in your estate plan money to take of the cost of raising Daisy and Duchess. Time-well it is something none of have enough of- but hopefully your caretaker for Daisy and Duchess will be willing to devote the time to provide Daisy and Duchess a happy and loving home.

Why do you not plan for the care of Daisy and Duchess? I have found the reasons for not planning for Daisy and Duchess to be similar to the reasons that you do not plan for your own family. The reasons I hear for not planning are:

- Procrastination-I know we should do it, but we are so busy;
- Not wanting to talk about death;
- Not recognizing that incapacity from disease or a traumatic event is a real possibility;
- It cost too much;
- My kids will take care of my pets;
- If they go to a shelter it will be for a short time and someone will adapt them; and
- I will outlive my pets.

The reality is life is uncertain. We don't know if and when we will become incapacitated. We don't know when we will die. We cannot say for certain we will outlive Daisy and Duchess. The time to plan is now, not when an event has occurred and the chance to care for you loved ones-family and pets- are gone.

How Can an Estate Planning Attorney Help You Plan for Daisy and Duchess?

I always tell my clients that we have to review the facts of their situation, understand their values, determine any special situations, decide who will make financial and medical decision when they cannot make them, and provide a plan for their specific needs when they die. It is no different for planning for Duchess and Daisy, you must decide who will make living decisions, who will make medical decisions, and who will handle finances for the care of Daisy and Duchess. Each situation is unique and requires prior planning.

For pet owners wanting to plan ahead for the care of their pets when they are gone, many states have provided for the establishment of pet trusts. In Oregon, the Oregon Pet Trust law provides a method to set up a special pet trust to manage money for and the care of your pets during their lifetime when you are gone. The trust lasts until the death of your pet, or if you have more than one pet, until the death of your second pet. Oregon will enforce a valid Trust. It doesn't matter if it's a Revocable Living Trust, a Life Insurance Trust or a Pet Trust. A Pet Trust, just like any other Trust must not only be created, but it must be funded. In other words, you must have cash transferred at your death into the Trust to provide for the care and maintenance of your Daisy and Duchess.

Daisy and Duchess Will Thank You for Providing For Their Future by Planning Who Will Care for Them

Who is Going to Take Care of Daisy and Duchess?

The first step is deciding who will care for your pets after you have gone. We refer to this person as the "*Caregiver*". Just as a *Caregiver* for a minor child is responsible for how the child is raise when you are gone, the pet Caregiver will take care of the everyday care of Daisy and Duchess. This person will determine if your pets need to be groomed, need vitamins, stay indoors or outdoors, and when they go to the vets.

I advise clients to talk with several people to determine who would make the best *Caregiver* for Daisy and Duchess. It could be family, but it does not have to be a relative. Also, when I set up a an estate plan for my human clients, when they name an Executor, Trustee, or Medical Agent, we also look for a backup in case the person you name is unable or unwilling to assume responsibility when the time come. You should have a back-up in mind for Daisy and Duchess.

Who is Going to Manage the Money for the Care of Daisy and Duchess?

Most people will set aside a fund of money for the care of their pet. You second decision is who is going to manage the money? This person will handle the money, and see that it is spent on Daisy and Duchess as you have directed in you Trust instructions. The Caregiver and the Trustee can be the same person. But you can also name two different people for each position. Just as with the Caregiver, you want to a backup person if the person you select is unable or willing to serve as Trustee.

The content of the Trust can vary, but an experienced

estate planning attorney can identify those items you should consider putting in your Pet Trust and help you draft your Trust to meet your specific needs as well as your State's law. Always include a provision for the immediate possession of your pet by the Caregiver.

Are You Ready For Emergencies?

Whatever happens to you will most likely occur suddenly. Whether it is incapacity or death, someone may need to jump in and take care of Daisy and Duchess immediately. What are some of the things you can do now to prepare for an emergency so your Daisy and Duchess are not forgotten and isolated? At a minimum I would:

- ✓ *Post emergency instructions* at home. The old magnet on the refrigerator might work for these instructions;
- ✓ *Get a pet card and keep it in your purse or wallet.* If you collapse in the parking lot and cannot talk, someone will alerted to the fact that Daisy and Duchess are at home and need immediate help and care;
- ✓ Make sure you *leave sufficient water* where your pets can get to it in case in all the confusion it is more than one day before someone reaches Daisy and Duchess; and
- ✓ **Give a neighbor or close family member a copy of the emergency instructions**.

There are several alternatives for an estate plan to take

care of your Daisy and Duchess when you cannot. If I had to decide what lawyer to discuss planning needs for Daisy and Duchess with, I would want an attorney that is sensitive to the needs of pet owners. He or she will explain how you can structure your plan so that your pet can be provided for immediately, not only if you die, but if you become ill or incapacitated. If you set up a trust fund for the care of your pet, it should only cost a few hundred dollars if you do it at the same time you draw up your estate plan. You can put the facts of the care of your pets in a Will, but that only provides for your pet in the case of your death and not if you are seriously ill or incapacitated. A **Pet Trust** is usually a better alternative.

How Much Money Should I Leave For Daisy and Duchess?

As with many things in life, the answer is it depends. When deciding how much to leave for Daisy and Duchess consider:

- The age of your pet;
- The cost of vet care in your part of the country;
- The number of pets;
- Any special medical conditions;
- The current standard of living;
- The need for kennel care during vacations; and
- Any special dietary needs.

I have seen amounts left from $6,000 to $10,000 dollars per pet. However, there is no minimum or maximum. If the amount is too large, it can trigger a Will or Trust challenge in court and use up valuable assets that could go to your loved ones and for the care of your pets.

The reality is, that for many of us who dearly love our Daisy and Duchess, they will outlive us and we will no longer be there to care for them and protect them. If something happens to us, there is more than one way to care for our beloved pets. Discuss your options with an experienced estate planning attorney so that you know Daisy and Duchess will survive your death.

CHAPTER 15

HELPING YOUR CHILD OR GRANDCHILD AFFORD THE COLLEGE OF THEIR CHOICE

Grandparents can leave a legacy by assisting with the educational expenses of grandchildren and may obtain some tax benefits in the process. While there are many options, this chapter addresses the advantages and disadvantage of 529 plans, Coverdell Education Savings Accounts, direct payment of tuition expenses, and the use of trusts.

529 Plans

529 plans are state-sponsored programs that are beneficial for and favored by grandparents who need to reduce their taxable

estate. In 2017, each grandparent can contribute up to $14,000 per year without paying gift taxes. There is no federal deduction available for contributions. Another benefit is federal tax free earnings on contributions.

There are two types of 529 plans. First, there are the investment plans. Investment choices are somewhat limited in these plans, which are often managed by large financial firms. If for some reason you need to get your money back, that is possible. You would have to pay the taxes and a 10% penalty on the gain on the assets in the plan. Also, you can change the beneficiary at any time. There is still uncertainty regarding how the funds in a 529 plan count for purposes of the grandchild qualifying for financial aid. Second, there are prepaid plans limited to certain private colleges. Each prepaid 529 plan has certain rules and investment guidelines.

The 529 plan has federal income tax advantages in that money contributed is tax-free and may be withdrawn tax-free for qualified college costs. For estate tax purposes, the value of the 529 account is not included in your gross estate. In 2017, you can contribute up to $14,000 tax free to a 529 plan. There is also a special five-year election that allows a $70,000 contribution for each child immediately.

The benefits of a 529 investment plan are that it provides professional management, allows a change in beneficiary to another qualified family member, and you maintain ownership and control of the account. You can even revoke the account at any time. The 529 plan is certainly an option you should consider for your child. You should also consider the disadvantages.

There are some disadvantages to the 529 plan. If distributions exceed qualifying college education costs, you will owe income tax and a 10% penalty on excess earnings. There is no penalty if the distribution is due to death or disability. 529 plans are run by the states and not the federal government. You have no control over how the state operates the plan or changes investment strategies. Your ability to switch among your 529 plan's investments is limited to once a year under the tax code.

Coverdell Education Savings Accounts (ESAs)

ESAs may be more advantageous for grandparents who have a large number of grandchildren or have limited funds to contribute to the ESA. With an ESA, subject to income limitations, you can contribute up to $2,000 for each child or grandchild annually. Beneficiaries must be under 18 when the contribution is made. Earnings on ESAs are usually not subject to federal income tax. They will be considered assets of the child or grandchild for purposes of calculating eligibility for financial aid. You determine how the funds are invested in an ESA. For example, you have the option to select stocks, bonds, CDs or mutual funds as an investment option. However, with an ESA, you cannot get your money back like you can with a 529 plan.

The annual limit per child or grandchild is $2,000. If a parent has contributed more than $2,000 to an ESA, excise taxes must be paid on the excess contributions.

The advantages of an ESA are that most types of investments qualify, ESA funds can be used for elementary and secondary schools as well as certain college expenses, and overall the ESA is simpler than a 529 to manage and stay compliant.

The disadvantages of an ESA are that the funds must be distributed by age 30, the funds must be for the exclusive use of the beneficiary, at age 30 the account terminates and any remaining funds are paid to the beneficiary and are subject to income tax and a 10% penalty.

Uniform Gift to Minors Act

Under the **Uniform Gift to Minors Act (UGMA)**, the accounts contain investments owned directly by your child or grandchild. Because minors are not allowed to hold investments directly, the account is placed under the control of a custodian subject to the UGMA or the Uniform Transfers to Minors Act. To set up an account, you can establish one at any financial institution and hold most types of financial assets such as stocks, bonds, CDs and mutual funds. Often grandparents make these gifts to reduce their estate taxes, although they can be subject to gift tax and generation-skipping transfer tax.

The advantages of a UGMA account is that grandparents

and parents can reduce their income taxes by shifting investment income from their higher income tax bracket to a child or grandchild's lower bracket. This would increase the investment return and provide more money for college. There is an income limitation on tax at the children's tax rate and annual investment income above the limit is taxed at the parents' marginal tax rate. A possible disadvantage of a UGMA account is that your child or grandchild upon obtaining direct ownership and control of any funds in the account does not have to use the money for college. If your goal was to provide for a college education for your child or grandchild, your goal may be defeated when your child or grandchild gets control of the account. Another potential disadvantage is that the funds in a UGMA account is counted in the determination of financial need for college.

Direct Payment of Tuition

Another option that is available to pay for your child's or grandchild's college and avoid gift and generation-skipping transfer tax is by making payment directly to the college. Only payments for tuition, not other expenses such as room and board, will qualify. A disadvantage of the direct payment strategy is that you will have to be alive when the child or grandchild is going to college in order to make the tuition payments directly. Also, to the extent that you make direct tuition payments, for financial aid purposes, most schools treat direct tuition payments as an asset-reducing financial aid.

Use of Trust to Provide for College Education

There are both advantages and disadvantages to establishing a trust for a grandchild or for multiple beneficiaries to create a fund to use for college expenses. One of the benefits in establishing a trust is that the assets contributed to the trust, including any appreciation in those assets, are removed from your taxable estate. Further, using the trust option, the funds can be used for college expenses or any other purposes. However, for financial aid purposes, a trust is usually considered the child's asset and will reduce the amount of financial aid available.

Care must be used in making gifts to the grandchild's trust because contributions are considered taxable gifts. However, in 2017, you can eliminate gift taxes by using your annual exclusion of $14,000, or $28,000 per recipient for gifts by married couples, or by applying the gift against your lifetime exclusion.

There are some technical requirements in using gifts in trust for your grandchildren to change the future interest to a present interest so it is a completed gift that is no longer in your estate. Usually this is done by a process that requires notification to the beneficiaries of a right to withdraw whenever a gift is made to the trust. When this is done, annual exclusion amount gifts to the trust are gift-tax and generating-skipping tax-free.

Title 2503 Minors Trust

Another option for a trust often used is what is called a Section 2503(c) Minors Trust. Contributions to the 2503(c) Minors Trust qualify as annual exclusion gifts even though they are gifts of a future interest, provided that: (1) the trust assets and income may be paid to or on behalf of the minor before age 21; (2) undistributed assets and income are paid to the minor at age 21; and (3) if the minor dies before reaching age 21, the trust assets will be included in his or her estate.

Deciding on which type of college savings vehicle to use is challenging. Consideration needs to be given to both the financial aspects of college savings as well as the estate plan effect on parents or grandparents.

CHAPTER 16

PLANNING FOR INDIVIDUALS WITH DISABILITIES WITH SPECIAL NEEDS TRUSTS OR ABLE ACCOUNTS

Special Persons-Special Needs

Special planning is required for individuals with special needs. This is one of the most complex areas of estate planning. It is impossible to cover all the issues and possible solutions for individuals with special needs. Further, this is a rapidly changing area of the law so any specifics outlined in this chapter, could be out dated in a few weeks or a few months. This chapter will give you an understanding of two options to provide supplemental benefits to an individual receiving government means tested benefits without losing those benefits. This chapter is limited to a discussion of special needs trusts and Able Accounts.

The Purpose of Special Needs Trusts

The overriding goal of a **Special Needs Trust ("SNT")** is protect assets of the disabled person while preserving the disabled person's right to receive government means based benefits. Simply stated, assets in a SNT are not counted in determining a disabled person's right to means based government benefits. SNTs are only for disabled persons receiving means tested benefits. No means tested benefits, no need for a SNT.

The two significant means tested benefits are: 1) Supplemental Security Income; and 2) Medicaid. Supplemental Security Income is a federal program to the disabled that is based on financial need. Currently a qualifying individual receives $733 for an individual and $1100 for a couple. The great benefit of Supplemental Security Income is anyone receiving it qualifies for Medicaid. To qualify, an individual cannot have more than $2,000 in 2016 in countable income. In addition, the individual cannot have more than the federal benefit rate in income in any month.

The second significant benefit is Medicaid, which provides health insurance to disabled low income individuals. This is important to a disabled person, because his or her condition can require unusually high medical care with a related high cost of care.

What Type of Special Needs Trust Do You Need?

First, review the benefits being received by the disabled person to determine if a SNT is appropriate. If it is appropriate, then there are only two choices for a SNT, First Party SNT and Third Party SNT. The two most important distinguishing features of a First and Third Party SNT is where do the funds come from and when the disabled person dies, does the estate have to pay the government? First party SNTs are funded with the disabled person's money and third part SNTs are funded with money from anyone other than the disabled person.

Key Elements of Third Party Special Needs Trust

The following elements are required in order to establish and maintain a third part SNT:

- Must be funded by money from anyone other than the disabled person;
- Any funds left in trust do not have to be paid to the government for benefits received when the disabled person dies;
- Can be created and funded at any age;
- Can be a testamentary SNT funded on the death of the person such as a parent who created the trust in his or her planning documents;
- Can be inter vivos SNT created and funded during the creator's lifetime and can also be funded after death;
- Can use a more flexible distribution standard than a first party trust;

- Distribution standard can be a strict- distribution standard for special needs only and not basic needs distribution;
- Distribution standard can also be a hybrid standard which includes distributions for food and housing; and
- Upon the death of the disabled person, any remaining funds will be distributed to beneficiaries as provided for in the trust document.

Key Elements of First Party Special Needs Trust

The following elements must be present for a first party SNT:

- Must be funded by money and assets from the disabled person;
- Must be established by parent, grandparent, guardian, conservator or the Court;
- Any funds left in trust must be paid back to the government for benefits received when the disabled person dies;
- Must be created and funded while the disabled person is under age 65;
- Can be a testamentary SNT funded on the death of the person such as a parent who created the trust in his or her planning documents;
- Can be inter vivos SNT created and funded during the creator's lifetime and can also be funded after death;
- Can use a more flexible distribution standard than a first party trust;

- Distribution standard can be a strict- distribution standard for special needs only and not basic needs distribution;
- Distribution standard can also be a hybrid standard which includes distributions for food and housing, but some states such as Oregon have objected to the use of a hybrid standards; and
- Upon the death of the disabled person, any remaining funds will be distributed to beneficiaries as provided for in the trust document.

The ABLE Act-Another Option for the Special Needs Person

Families with a special needs person have traditionally relied on a Special Needs Trust to provide for the member's standard of living needs not covered by means tested government benefits. Fewer people who come to me for estate planning services have heard of a federal law that allows states to create a program of savings for a certain segment of the disabled population without losing their right to means based government benefits. The Achieving a Better Life Experience, or "ABLE Act" provides an alternative method of funding for parents, relatives and third parties to fund a disabled persons supplemental lifestyle needs. Once a state starts the program, any third person can contribute to an ABLE account for the disabled person and in Oregon receive an Oregon tax credit. Oregon established its ABLE program which was operational in December 2016.

What are the Key Provisions of the Oregon ABLE Act?

Not all states have ABLE programs. Check with your 529 account administrator to see if your State has an ABLE program. While the details of each state's ABLE accounts will vary, in a nutshell, as an example, here are the Oregon Able account key features:

- A person must be diagnosed with a disability **before** the age of 26;
- Government means based benefit eligibility is not lost as long as the amount of contributions are under $100,000;
- $14,000, the annual gift tax exclusion amount can be contributed to an ABLE account each year;
- Investment earnings grow tax-deferred;
- Qualified disability expense payments are tax free;
- In 2016 contributions to are tax deductible up to $2,310 for single filers and $4,620 for joint filers if the beneficiary is under 21;
- ABLE accounts can be used to pay for housing, transportation, education, financial management, and health expenses with tax free distributions;
- The Oregon ABLE account savings limit is $310,000;
- The Oregon ABLE account up to $100,000 is exempted from the SSI $2,000 asset limit;
- Suspension of SSI benefits- An ABLE account balance in excess of $100,000;
- At termination there is a **payback of benefits** to the government;

- Oregon ABLE accounts have a choice of investments; and
- Investment choices can be changed up to twice a year.

Who is Eligible for an Oregon ABLE Account?

A disabled person is eligible for an ABLE account if:

- Start of disability- **before 26**;
- Automatic eligibility-If you meet the disability onset requirement and receive SSI or SSDI benefits; and
- Doctor certification- If you do not meet other requirements- you will need doctor's certification of significant functional limitation.

Within the Guidelines ABLE Accounts Will Not Affect Eligibility for Means Tested Benefits

Eligibility for means tested public benefits require that at the current time an individual have assets valued at less than $2,000. Savings up to $100,000 in ABLE accounts provide a safe harbor and will not affect eligibility for public benefits.

Choosing Between a Special Needs Trust or ABLE Account?

Families with special needs members have long relied on the Special Needs Trust as estate planning technique for providing funds to supplement government benefits. A Special

Needs Trust is a trust funded with assets under the management and control of a trustee, a fiduciary, who is directed to manage the trust assets for the benefit of the person with a disability.

This used to be the only way to save money for a disabled person without losing government benefits. The Special Needs Trust provided assets for care above the level of government benefits. The Special Needs Trust is funded by life time gifts, and at death by life insurance or inheritances. Some forms of Special Needs Trusts require government payback and others do not.

Factors to Consider in Choosing Special Needs Trust or ABLE Account

When comparing a Special Needs Trust and an ABLE account you must consider that both are intended to give disabled individuals the ability to save while protecting their government benefits. With that objective in mind, here are some factors to consider in making your decision whether to use a Special Needs Trust or an ABLE account:

- **Cost:** The Special Needs Trust will generally cost more to establish and is more complicated than an ABLE account. The ABLE account is usually easier to establish, funds grow tax free, and is usually less costly to establish;
- **Eligibility for Benefits**: Both will protect benefits for the individual with disability, but if drafted incorrectly the Special Needs Trust could defeat eligibility. An ABLE account is only available to someone who sustained a disability prior to age 26 and if over funded results in suspension of benefits;

- **Medicaid Payback**: A pooled and a first party Special Needs Trust require a Medicaid payback. A third party Special Needs Trust does not require a payback. ABLE accounts are all Medicaid payback accounts;
- **Contribution Limit**: There is no contribution limit for the Special Needs Trust. The contributions to a Special Needs Trust are tax free regardless of source or amount. An ABLE account is limited to annual contributions of $14,000 and a maximum of $100,000 before suspension of government benefits; and
- **Death of Beneficiary**: If a third party Special Needs Trust is used the remaining funds are paid to the family members. Under an ABLE account and a first party Special Needs Trust all Medicaid benefits are required to be paid back.

The personal financial situation of the individual will determine which option is the most beneficial. Whether a Special Needs Trust or an ABLE account is better in a particular situation will depend on all the facts, special circumstances, the Oregon ABLE program, and the desire for control or third party management. There is no right answer that fits all situations.

CHAPTER 17

PERSONAL RESIDENCE PLANNING-HOW TO HAVE YOUR CAKE (PERSONAL RESIDENCE) AND EAT IT TOO

4 Options for Baby Boomers to Stay in Their Home during Retirement

Retirement planning was a lot simpler thirty years ago when I started practicing law. Usually seniors getting ready to retire had a savings account, a pension plan from their employer, and there home was paid for or close to paid off. The decision to stay in their home or to move, was based on non-economic factors such as a personal attachment to their home or neighborhood, a cadre of personal friends they may have known for years, children living nearby, whether the home is too large to keep up both inside and outside, and the climate.

Today, retirement for our current Baby Boomer generation is entirely different. Today most retiring Baby Boomers I see do not have a company pension. Instead they have an IRA or 401K or PERS retirement plan, partially or fully funded by their own savings. Some have life insurance policies, but few have long term care insurance or any plan to take care of long term care needs. Probably a majority no longer have a home that is free and clear of a mortgage. Today's Baby Boomers now have to make hard economic and non-economic decisions when it becomes time to retire. One very important decision is whether to stay in their home.

What if you want to stay in your home, but cash flow or monthly income is border line or even appears not to support your desire to stay in your home? If you really want to stay in your home, and are willing to take some financial risks there are solutions. One solution is a reverse mortgage. The lender pays off your current mortgage and does not collect on the reverse mortgage until you no longer live in the house. Another strategy is to sell your home at the market value to your children and rent from them. Another alternative is to sell to your children at a discount. If estate taxes are an issue for you and you would like to stay in your home while reducing estate taxes then you can transfer your house to a **Qualified Personal Residence Trust ("QPRT")**. Under a QPRT you stay in your home for a set number of years. After the term of the Trust is over, you then rent from your beneficiaries, usually your children.

The Good, Bad and Ugly of Reverse Mortgages

We see on television well know actors pitching the wonders of reverse mortgages for seniors who want to live in their homes during their retirement years. Are reverse mortgages for every senior? No. They benefit some, but are not for every senior.

Reverse mortgage can be a benefit for those seniors who have for whatever reason failed to accumulate enough assets to generate sufficient income to meet their living expenses, including their home mortgage, tax and insurance payments in retirement. A reverse mortgage can be a solution to stay in your home and to free up cash flow for your retirement living needs. Instead of large home equity to leave your children, you have cash to live on during your retirement years.

Who might not want a reverse mortgage? If you do not want to live in your home for a significant number of years, either by choice, health, or family concerns, you probably will not benefit from a reverse mortgage. Like any other home loan a reverse mortgage has costs. A reverse mortgage has all the cost of any other mortgage you might take out when you bought the home such a lender fees, appraisals, inspections, escrow, title, transfer fees, and the many other fees lenders and others with creative minds can think to charge. If you are only going to live in the house a few years that does not give you enough time to gain reduced cash outflow to offset the cost of the mortgage.

In a nutshell, a reverse mortgage trades your home equity for cash. Unlike a regular mortgage, you do not make payments during your lifetime. The loan is repaid when you no longer live in the home, either through sale, failure to pay taxes and insurance, or by death. Once you no longer use the home as a personal residence the loan is due and the loan must be paid off by cash, refinance, or sale of the property. To obtain a reverse mortgage the youngest borrower has to be 62, you must have a certain amount of equity in the home, and you must be able to pay taxes, insurance and maintenance, and live in the home.

The Good-Benefits of Reverse Mortgage

You are a senior 62 and over and you are considering a reverse mortgage to improve your retirement living and to stay in the home you have lived in for years. What can a reverse mortgage do for you?

- You can stay in your home as long as you want, even up to the death of a surviving spouse;
- You convert what is currently a monthly payment on an existing mortgage to a no principal and interest payment reverse mortgage;
- You reduce your payment of principal, interest, taxes and insurance to payment of only tax and insurance;
- With or without a reverse mortgage you still pay property expenses for maintenance and homeowner's association;

- Depending on the amount of your equity, you may receive payments for expenses and emergencies;
- It doesn't matter what the value of your home is when you die, the lender is paid the proceeds of the sale up to the loan principal plus accrued interest and expenses, you children are not liable if the loan balance exceeds the proceeds of the sale;
- If the home value is greater than the loan balance your heirs or children inherit the home, can sell it or refinance the loan and keep the house, and benefit from any cash remaining;
- When the reverse mortgage is made, there is no tax on payment of the cash proceeds; and
- The interest rate is usually near market rate.

The Bad- The Risks and Disadvantages of Reverse Mortgages

Like any other product or strategy in estate planning, a reverse mortgage has its disadvantages.

- The costs can be higher than a conventional mortgage. One additional fee is the mortgage insurance which guarantees payment of the loan. Because the home value could be upside down to the loan value, the lender is protected by the mortgage insurance;
- Interest is not paid as accrued as on a regular mortgage, but is added to the loan balance causing the balance to grow over time and reduce your equity;

- If you stay in the house a long time, the loan balance may exceed the value and reduce the current inheritance of your children;
- Many seniors, due to health issues, qualify for means based government benefits. The rules on means based benefits change frequently and may affect means based benefits;
- If you move before you die, you have to repay the loan.

Selling You Home to Your Children at Fair Market Value Can Provide a Way to Stay in Your Home or Freeze Out of Your Estate Future Appreciation

A second strategy is to sell your home to your children at fair market value (same price a third person would pay) and let your children pay for it with an installment note. You can then rent it at fair market value or your child can move into the home. In this case if you do everything right, you can probably remove the home from your estate, receive a cash flow, and help your children to build equity and refinance the home. The key elements to this strategy are:

- Transfer your home to your children at full market value;
- Provide an installment note for your children to finance the purchase;
- You receive monthly payments while you are alive on the installment note which is secured by the real estate;

- The installment note carries an interest rate determined by the federal rate in the Revenue Bulletin up to the market rate of interest;
- Tax deduction for mortgage interest and property taxes are deductible for the children purchasing the house;
- Do not forgive payments, but if you want you can make separate tax free annual gifts of up to $14,000 in 2017 to your child;
- You can take your tax exemption in effect in the year of sale of a personal residence to avoid any capital gains tax;
- You will be responsible for income tax on the interest received on the installment note;
- There should be no gift tax on the sale because you sold the property at fair market value, same as if you sold it to a third party; and
- Future appreciation of your home is not in your estate, but is value included in your children's estate.

Obviously, this is a strategy that should be accomplished with professional help to make sure it complies with all tax requirements. The primary benefit is reduction of capital gains tax to the parents, increased cash flow to the parents, and eliminating future appreciation from the parent's estate.

The disadvantage is that the children pick up an obligation for which the note payments may be greater than they can afford when combined with tax and insurance payments creating a negative cash flow. Also, the children do not have the flexibility to sell the property, at least not in a practical sense, while their parents are alive. Further, if they do sell within two years any gain will be taxed to the parents.

Using this technique requires a very frank family discussion to make sure all parties are on board before, a visit to a lawyer to put the deal together. The other consideration is the cost. It will require the services of a lawyer. Not only one lawyer, but two. The children and parents should not be represented by the same attorney, just as they would not be represented by the same attorney in any arms-length market sale of real estate.

A Bargain Sale of the House to Your Family Can Trigger Negative Tax Consequences

A third option to stay in your house and transfer it to a child or other family member is through a sale at a bargain price. In most cases I have seen, this is not a good idea. The major problem with this strategy is taxes. The IRS treats this as a two-step transaction with tax consequences to both steps. Let's call these steps the sale step and the gift step.

The Sale Step

The sale step where the parent's family home is sold to a child at a bargain price. In this step, the parent's cost basis in the property is used to calculate capital gains that is applied to the bargain sale price. The amount of the gift, the difference between the fair market value and the bargain price, will result in a gift and may be subject to a gift tax.   Depending on the size of the parent's estate, the amount of the gift, the gift tax exemption amount in the year of the sale, and the prior gifts made by the parents, this type of transaction may or may not be beneficial to the parents. The sale will generate a capital gains tax, but the parent's probably will be able to use the homeowner tax exemption to offset this gain and avoid payment of any capital gains tax.

The Gift Step

Step two, the gift step, will trigger a gift of the difference between the bargain sale price and the fair market value price. The gift tax implications will vary with each individual situation.

This strategy can be very helpful to the parents who want to pass the family home to their children and either rent the home from the children or provide a home to the children, while the parents move elsewhere. In contrast, this transaction can create tax problems for the children that should be addressed in structuring the transaction. Ideally, the children will move in the house and after living there for two years will receive the benefit of the homeowner tax exemption if they thereafter sell the home.

Qualified Personal Residence Trust to Stay in Your Home-Know the Risks

A *Qualified Personal Residence Trust ("QPRT")* is an estate planning and tax planning strategy that can reduce estate taxes and remove future appreciation from your estate, while providing a method of allowing you to stay in your home. In return, you give up control to your children and expand your risks of homeownership to include the financial risks encountered by your children.

Can You Live in an Irrevocable Trust?

A QPRT is an Irrevocable Trust drafted to comply with the requirements of the IRS regulations. Those requirements require that:

- The QPRT is irrevocable;
- The only asset in the QPRT is your home;
- The QPRT is created for a specified number of years; and
- If it is your home that funds the QPRT for the strategy to work you must live in the home as your personal residence for the term of the QPRT.

How to Implement the QPRT Strategy

The short version of a complicated strategy is:

- Transfer your home to the QPRT;
- Live in the home during the term rent free;
- The Parents cannot have the right to purchase the house;
- Parents pay tax, insurance and minor repairs;
- Parents stay alive longer than the term of the QPRT;
- The children get the home at the end of the term of the QPRT;

- After the expiration of the QPRT term the parents can rent from the children at fair market rent; and
- If the house is no longer used as a personal residence, the QPRT Trustee must either distribute assets to parents or convert the QPRT to a grantor retained annuity trust.

These requirements must be adhered to for the tax benefits available under the IRS regulations. Many people shy away from this strategy when they learn that the strategy will not work if they die or move from the property within the term of the QPRT and that there children are going to be their landlords. This strategy should only be used with the advice of a qualified estate planning or tax attorney.

The Benefits of a QPRT

The QPRT provides the following benefits to the parents.

- A QPRT is easy to create with professional assistance;
- The QPRT if drafted properly is recognized by the IRS;
- Removal of the value of the personal residence from their estate;
- Removal of future appreciation of your personal residence from the value of your estate;
- Parents can live in the personal residence during the term rent free;
- Parents during the term can take income tax deductions of ownership;
- If estate tax rates increase in the future, the value of your personal residence can escape this increase at the conclusion of the term;

- Transfer of the personal residence to the children at the end of the term;
- Staying in the house without rent for the term and then renting from the children at the market rate after the term;
- No loss of the unified tax credit if the parents survive the term;
- Further reduction of the estate by payment of taxes during the term by the parents; and
- If primary residence the parents can benefit from the capital gain exclusion when the primary residence is sold during the QPRT term.

QPRTs are Not for Everyone

As mentioned above candidates for a QPRT often reject the technique for non-tax reasons such as having to live in the personal residence for the term of the QPRT and not wanting their children to be in control. Here is a list of the potential disadvantages of a QPRT.

- At the end of the trust period the children become landlords and parents are not comfortable with that situation;
- If the children sell the personal residence there might be a significant income tax liability because if the parents survive the term, there is no stepped-up tax basis;
- This technique is difficult to implement if the personal residence has a secure mortgage on the property;

- It can be difficult to sell the personal residence during the QPRT term due to tax consequences;
- There will be costs to create and maintain the QPRT to comply with regulations including legal, accounting and appraisal fees;
- If the parents die during the term of the QPRT, the trust terminates and the personal residence reverts back to the parent's estate; and
- No Generation Skipping Tax planning is effective until the end of the term.

Don't Try This at Home

We often associate this warning with high risk events or dangerous procedures. It also applies to using a QPRT. Before moving forward with this strategy make sure it will work for your situation. Make sure you understand how a QPRT works, the benefits and the disadvantages before using this estate planning strategy for your personal residence.

In summary, there are multiple options to consider if you are currently a Baby Boomer who would like to stay in your house in retirement, but don't quite have the cash flow to remain in the house. While the ideal solution might be to stay put and continue to pay your mortgage, your circumstances may dictate a more favorable course of action for your situation. The above are four options you might consider. However, other options exist, only limited by the creativity of your advisor and your risk/reward make up.

CHAPTER 18

HOW LIKELY IS IT THAT YOU WILL NEED LONG TERM CARE SERVICES?

70% of Today's Baby Boomers Will Need Long Term Care-Are You Ready?

How many people become 65 year old Baby Boomers each day? According to government statistics, an average of 10,000 baby boomers turn 65 each and every day. While today's 65 year olds are healthier than the prior generation, age related mental illness and physical decline will come, just later in life than for their parents. It is estimated that 40% of the Baby Boomers who turn 65 will at some point need a nursing home and 70% will need in home care. The odds are against a Baby Boomer not needing either a nursing home or in home care.

While we think of long term care for seniors, long term care can be a necessity for younger people. Think about it, do you know someone who was injured at work, was hurt at home working in the yard or on home maintenance, or was in a major automobile accident. It is just like people I talk to who put off making a Will or Trust and doing their Estate Planning because they are young and don't expect incapacity or death until they are seniors. It is always going to happen to the other person. The reality is we don't know when incapacity will hit and you will need long term care.

How Much Does Long Term Care Service Costs?

In a word-**expensive**. For example, according to a study by **Genworth,** in 2016 the national average cost for a private nursing home was $89,060, for a semi-private nursing home room $80,574, for an assisted living facility $47,400, and home care costs about $ 58,236. In the 2016 study for a state like Oregon that has an average cost of living, the average cost for nursing home care is depending on private of semi-private room: $101,100-$107, 316.

The average time a person is in a facility is about 30 months. In Oregon, a nursing home stay would cost a family about $250,000. Most people are lucky to have that amount in their retirement savings. You work your whole life to pay for less than three years of living. It doesn't seem fair. Very few people I know are able to pay these expenses.

If You Have Aging Parents What are the Options for Caring for Them When Cannot Take Care of Themselves?

I have experienced three different options with my grandmother, mother, and close friend. I can talk from experience about the options of living at home, living with family, and living in an assisted living facility. Many of my estate planning clients now live with family or in assisted living facilities. Each option can be expensive, some double the cost of others. On the other hand, each option places a burden and stress on the family. However, once a Baby Boomer reaches the point they can no longer manage on their own, the choice is not if long term care is needed, but what is the best option for long term care. The basic options are:

- **Living at Home**. When the person cannot take care of all needs, but can handle some, they may be able to live at home. Family members must come frequently to perform functions such as providing medication, bathing, preparation of food, running errands and doctor visits, and taking care of the house and yard.
- **Living in Senior House with Family Member Aid**. A family member moves in and devotes his or her life to caring for the senior. The house may need to be modified for handicapped and money may need to be paid to care givers to relieve the family member.

- **Move to Home of Family Member**. This defeats the goal of staying in your home until death. Also, the family member home may not be large enough or set up for a disabled person.
- **Home Health Care Provider.** This care can range from help a few hours a week to full time health care. If extensive care is needed, the cost can be prohibitive. I know several years ago when I looked at this option for my mother, the cost was around $6,000 per month. She was at a point that she needed extensive care around the clock and family could only provide limited time due to their work schedules to reduce the paid care giver services.
- **Assisted Living Facility**. This works if the senior is still mobile and can manage to care for some of her daily needs. Food is prepared, basic needs are provided on site, and full time staff provides health care. Again, this is expensive, but does relieve some of the family stress.
- **Nursing Home.** This is usually the last step and requires constant observation and care. It is the most expensive of the options.

What are the Options to Pay for Long Term Care Services?

There are limited options to pay for long term care. However, for the vast majority of people they have to rely sooner or later on Medicaid. Further, some of the options are limited, such as a person has to be 65 or older or a veteran. Others, such as Medicaid, are designed for people with limited assets. Because today's Baby Boomers are either without resources or will be when the need for care arises, over 50% of today's long term care is paid for by Medicaid. Briefly , the sources for payment of long term care are: 1) Medicare-pays limited amounts for limited time for home health care; 2) Veteran's Benefit- for veteran and spouse who served during war time provides limited assistance in form of income for care in nursing home; 3) Long term care insurance- it has many different forms and options, so it may cover a large percentage of the cost, or be of little help depending on the policy purchased; 4) Current Income and Savings- at the highest level of cost, assets can be gone in less than three years; and 5) Medicaid-can be used if the person is blind, permanently and totally disabled, or over 65 and needs long term care; meets the income limit; and as countable assets of only $2,000 or less.

The Primary Source of Funding for Long Term Care Services-Medicaid

Medicaid is by far the primary source of funding for long term care services for the majority of recipients. If you are like most people, your life long economic goal was not to work all your life to qualify for Medicaid, but the reality is qualifying for Medicaid may be the only way to pay for long term care and with proper advanced planning preserve assets for your family.

Medicaid provides diverse services. In Oregon it covers health insurance and long term care services for low asset, low income individuals.

Medicaid Eligibility

Individuals with long term care needs can qualify for Medicaid support based on three factors:

- Disability;
- Resources; and
- Income.

Step 1-Disability Determination

The first step is qualifying for Medicaid assistance for long term care services is an assessment by the State agency. This assessment in most states concentrates on whether the individual can perform the activities of daily living. Those activities include:

- Eating;
- Dressing and Grooming;
- Bathing and Personal Hygiene;
- Mobility, Ambulation and Transfer;
- Elimination; and
- Cognition and Behavior.

There are several criteria used for this evaluation including performance over a 30 day look back period and 30 day look forward period, comparison with actual needs, and current function without assistance. In Oregon, the individual is then rated on a score of 1 to 18 with each level determinative of a certain level of service or non-service. The State will reevaluate the individual's needs every 12 months. Basically, a requalification for assistance.

Step 2-Resource Qualification

Not only is income a factor in being eligible for Medicaid, but a person can only have limited *countable assets* to be eligible for Medicaid. This is where we have to have two buckets, the **"*available*"** bucket and the **"*non- available*"** bucket. Once we determine what is in the *"available"* bucket, then we have to have two separate boxes, the *"countable"* and the *"excluded"*. When we get to the *"countable"* box, we can then determine if Medicaid is available to the individual.

An asset goes into the *"available"* bucket if the individual, and if he or she is married his or her spouse, owns the asset. So far, simple enough. But wait, there are exceptions that go into the *"non-available"* bucket. In Oregon those items that go in the *"non-available"* bucket include:

- With limitations, if the asset is in an irrevocable trust and cannot be used for the individual's or spouse's basic needs;
- Assets used to avoid the risk of domestic violence or to avoid an abusive situation;
- Joint ownership and joint owner is unwilling to sell their interest;

- The individual owns an asset, but is unable to gain possession; and
- The individual owns an asset but is incompetent to gain possession.

We have identified what goes into the *"available"* bucket. Now we have to divide the *"available"* bucket into the *"**excluded**"* box and the *"**countable**"* box. It is only what gets to the *"countable"* box that is included in determining Medicaid benefit eligibility.

Excluded?

Excluded assets are determined by the then existing rule of the respective State. Each State will have its own set of rules as to what is excluded. There are limitations on use, amount, and other requirements for an asset to be excluded, but the following is a list of potentially excluded assets if all the requirements of the State rules are followed:

- Home;
- Car;
- Personal Belongings;
- Burial Arrangements;
- Burial space;
- Life Insurance with restrictions;
- Pensions and Retirement plans that only allow periodic payments;

- Qualified annuities;
- Equity in real property other than the home; and
- Income in the month of receipt.

Note that there are many restrictions, qualifications and exceptions to each of the above *"excluded"* items. You must read the regulations carefully and make sure each item meets the requirements of the regulations. In Oregon these rules are found in Oregon Administrative Rules 461-145. These rules change frequently and are complex. Do not rely on the above list and consult with an attorney if you are trying to determine eligibility for Medicaid benefits.

Countable?

What do we put in the "countable" box? If it is not in the *"excluded"* box, then it is in the *"countable"* box. In Oregon, at the current time, if an individual is single, the *"countable"* box limit is $2,000.

Step 3-Income Qualification

Each state defines *"income"* to be used to determine if an individual is eligible for Medicaid. The income limit in Oregon for example, is $2,199 in 2016. The regulations contain an extensive list of assets and how the income from those sources are classified to determine if they are part of the countable income for an individual. If after properly accounting for the income sources, the individual's income exceeds $2,199 he or she should consult with an estate and elder law attorney to determine if there is an available strategy to lower the income to qualify for Medicaid.

One planning option is an **Income Cap Trust**. The Income Cap Trust is a complex trust that must have certain provisions to qualify. The complete details are beyond the scope of this book. However, generally this is an irrevocable trust which receives all of the individuals monthly income, the Trustee distributes certain amounts for the benefit of the individual, and the balance of the income is used to pay for the individuals long term care expense. Medicaid will then pay for the unpaid balance of expenses. The regulations are very specific on the items and how much can be paid from the income each month.

The Penalty Period

Many people transfer assets to reduce the "countable" box to qualify for Medicaid. However, there is a look back period of five years for assets given away. The start date for the **penalty period** is when a person becomes eligible for Medicaid. The penalty period is calculated by dividing the amount of the gift by the monthly facility cost.

Estate Planning Should Include Long Term Care Planning

Estate planning is designed primarily to determine how a person will transfer his or her assets on death, plan for having decision makers in place in the case of incapacity, and have a medical agent in place to make medical and end of life decisions when you cannot make those decisions. Long term care planning involves what type of services would be needed if you lose your ability to take care of yourself based on the seven daily activities used by Medicaid.

While difficult to do before long term care is near, a key planning strategy that needs to be implemented at least five years prior to needing assistance is moving assets out of the "*countable*" box into the "*excluded*" box. To the extent you start a gifting program, you need to complete it prior to the five year look back period. You should also consider the use of an irrevocable trust. This trust must be both drafted and funded before the penalty period.

Long term care estate planning is filled with risk. You have to consider the look back penalty period, income levels which may require an income cap trust, and estate recoveries.

This chapter is a very brief introduction into long term care planning. This is a complex area of the law that most people lack adequate knowledge of to make informed decisions. Further, this is one area of the law that is constantly changing. This is an area of the law where you must establish a long term care plan and update that plan on a regular basis. This plan must not only include the legal aspects of your plan, but also you must work with family and friends on the practical side of how care will be provided and what will be the source of payment. You don't want to have worked all your life to pay for your rainy day-long term care.

CHAPTER 19

CHARITABLE GIVING

Is It Really Ours?

We go through life working hard, saving, accumulating wealth and trying to provide for our family. In addition to providing for our family during our lifetime, we want to make sure they are taken care of when we pass. We come into this world with nothing. We can take nothing with us when we leave this world. In short, we are only stewards over a group of assets while we are on this earth. Most people try to do with what they have been given, and share with others in need besides family members. When it comes to charity, even though we no longer own the assets after we die, we can still control how those assets are used and determine how to provide for more than our family. It may not be ours after we die, but we can control how our assets are used after we die.

Why Give to Charity or Church?

One main reason is to satisfy your desire to help those beyond your family. The second main reason is that the government provides tax incentives to make charitable gifts. Tax deductions are available for charitable gifts whether the gifts are during your lifetime or after death.

How Can You Give Money to Charity?

There are numerous methods to give money to charity. Some methods are simple such as an outright gift and others are complex such as a Charitable Remainder Trust. Some methods make sense for gifts under a specific value, while others because of their cost and complexity require donation in hundreds of thousands or even millions. Which method is right for your depends on your specific situation.

Six Methods to Make Charitable Donations and Receive Tax Benefits

This information provides a general overview to give you some background knowledge regarding charitable giving. Laws change frequently and states often treat transactions differently. With the information in this section you can discuss with an estate planning attorney your options and what is right for your situation. This information only provides a background for you so that you can have some knowledge of your options before discussing the details with a planner. This is a complex area of the law that is best accomplished with professional advice.

Gift

This is the simplest method and probably the most often used. Other methods such as Charitable Remainder Trust, Charitable Lead Trust, Private Annuities and Donor Advised Funds discussed later are usually for much larger donations and involve sophisticated tax planning. Outright gifts can be made during life or after death. Other than establishing a value on the property donated, there is not a lot of planning required. It can something as simple as a gift of cash now or leaving a part of your estate in your Will to your favorite charity.

You can even have a life insurance policy for a charitable organization. In order to receive the charitable tax deduction you must irrevocably assign your rights to the charity. There are differences in the requirements based on whether the policy is or is not paid in full.

What cannot be donated to charity are earmarked gifts-for a specific group of people- or S Corporation stock.

Charitable Annuity

The Charitable Annuity concept is simple. You transfer an asset to a charity and the charity promises to pay you or you and your spouse an annuity for you or your spouse's lifetime.   The annuity can be immediate or deferred. From a tax standpoint, the deferred annuity is usually advantageous to the donor. It can also be used as a retirement vehicle. The charity will go through a calculation and consider a number of factors in determining how much the annuity will pay each year.

In summary, the benefits of a Charitable Annuity are:

- Simple compared to Trusts;
- Secured by the assets and income of the Charity;
- Comparatively low cost to set up;
- Not subject to certain taxes that other methods are subject to pay;
- Can be funded with business partnership interest or closely held business stock; and
- S Corporation stock can be used for donation.

There are tax consequence that you will need to be aware of if you are establishing a Charitable Annuity. These include the potential for unrelated business taxable income, income tax treatment, gift tax cautions, and estate taxes. The scope of each of these tax implications is beyond this introductory chapter. However, the rules are complicated and a Charitable Annuity should only be set up with professional advice provide the most tax effective plan possible.

Charitable Remainder Trust

Another method to leave money for your favorite charity is through a Charitable Remainder Trust ("CRT"). In addition to cash, if you have an asset such as real estate, a closely held business, or shares of stock that you have had a long time and it has appreciated a CRT may be the method best suited for your charitable giving. You receive lifetime income and what is left in principal when you die goes to charity. You reduce income taxes now and estate taxes when you die. By using highly appreciated assets you can avoid capital gains tax on transferring real estate or stock.

In summary, the benefits of a CRT are:

- Convert highly appreciated assets into a lifetime income;
- Avoid the capital gains tax on appreciated assets when the asset is transferred to the CRT;
- Reduce estate taxes;
- Get a current charitable income tax deduction;
- IRS Specimen forms of Trusts; and
- Make a donation to your favorite charity upon your death.

The concept is simple, the implementation and paper work can be complex. Say you have a piece of rental real estate that has appreciated over the years. You transfer the rental house into an irrevocable trust. An irrevocable trust generally cannot be amended or changed except for certain limited provisions. This has the effect of removing the rental property from your estate, thus, eliminating estate tax on the value of the rental property. The Trustee of the CRT then sells the rental property. Once the rental property is sold, the Trustee takes the proceeds from the sale and invest it in an income producing asset. Say the proceeds of the rental property sale is $100,000. If the Trustee invests it to earn 5% then $5,000 per year would go to you. If the principal amount is still $100,000 at your death, then the proceeds would be transferred to the charity that you have chosen.

While in the above example we used a payout of the income for a fixed percentage which is a **unitrust.** The payout to you each year could fluctuate based on the principal amount and the investment results. The CRT assets grow tax free.

A second option is to pay you a fixed percentage return or the actual income of the CRT, whichever is less. This option is often used when the asset is hard to liquidate like a family business.

A third option is to receive fixed income each year regardless of performance. This is often referred to as an annuity trust. The annuity trust must pay out at least 5% but no more than 50% of the initial value of the trust asset. You will find older people wanting the fixed income option.

The income payments can be made to the person who set up the CRT and his or her spouse. If set up properly payments can continue until the second person dies. Other options exist such as paying income for a fixed period, paying income on the life of your children, or to another person if it meets certain IRS requirements. You can also defer taking any income payments and let the value of the CRT grow before drawing income.

There are limitations on the amount and timing of tax deductions. Because the CRT rules are complicated and frequently changing, the IRS has provided a number of specimen trusts depending on what your intent and goal is for the CRT. If you decide to set up a CRT, you will want to consult a professional to learn what the current law is with respect to terms of the CRT and tax rules.

Charitable Lead Trust

If you prefer to give the annual income from an asset to charity and leave the principal for your family or other individuals then you can set up a *Charitable Lead Trust ("CLT").* To obtain income, estate and gift tax deductions the charitable interest can only be one of two types of interest: 1) a *"guaranteed annuity"*; or 2) a *"unitrust."* Compared to a CRT discussed above the interest can be less than 5% of principal and there is no net income CLT *unitrust.*

For most people reading this they are probably saying what is he talking about? That is the reason you should not use a CLT without professional advice. For now, just understand this is an option if you want to leave principal to your beneficiaries when you die, but you want to give annually to charity while you are alive.

The tax treatment of CLT are also complicated. Before

setting up a CLT discuss the transfer tax implications, especially when the ultimate beneficiaries are family members, the estate tax inclusion, how the annual charitable deduction is calculated, and generation skipping tax consequences. CLTs are unique in that they are not tax-exempt.

The IRS provides specimen forms for a CLT. Not only does this provide a road map for the drafting of the CLT, but if the CLT follows the specimen CLT forms, is operated in compliance with the specimen CLT form and is valid under local law, the IRS will recognize the CLT for tax purposes.

Private Foundations

Private Foundations are used by higher net worth individuals so the discussion of Private Foundations will be brief. A Private Foundation provides a vehicle for control and flexibility in providing an ongoing charitable donation. However, Private Foundations are complex, can be subject to a penalty tax, and many procedural requirements. The administrative, tax and financial restrictions prevent most people and families from creating a Private Foundation.

Donor Advised Funds

Public charities who have control over how the money is used are called **Donor Advised Funds**. The Fund is a separate fund managed by a charity. The donor can make recommendations how the money should be used, put the foundation does not have to follow the recommendation. These funds are created by spent. Again the rules are complex and before any donation to a Donor Advised Fund, you should seek professional help.

FINAL THOUGHTS

FOUR TRUTHS:

- *We come into the world with nothing;*
- *We control our assets and property while we are here;*
- *We leave this world with no property; and*
- *We can control some of our assets and continue to do good after we leave this world.*

Many people who come to me have had a charitable gifting plan all their lives. Others as they consider who to care for with their property, feel a responsibility to the poor and needy in addition to their family. They often express the feeling that they have had a good life and are thankful that they could always provide for their family and would like to share the wealth that came from their labor with those that do not have the riches of life they had.

As you approach your estate plan, determine if including your church or a charitable organization, whether you donated during your life or not, is something you do want to do when you die. Your estate plan is not your only chance to donate to and care for the less fortunate and needy, but it is your last chance. We all want to care for our family first, but once that responsibility is met, do you want to leave a legacy?

There are three options for your estate plan:

- **Intestate**- Do not plan and let the State distribute your assets for you when you die. Let the Probate Court select your Personal Representative who will decide who gets your property and if you have minor children who will raise them;
- **Create a Will or Trust Plan**- You can determine who gets your property and how it will be divided. A Will or Trust plan usually provides for your family and goes no further; and

- **Create a Will or Trust Plan with Charitable Giving-** People who follow this plan have chosen to direct their property to where it can do the most good. They leave their property with their hearts. They provide an amount for their family that will meet their needs and then pass additional wealth to others in need through a church or charity.

You cannot take it with you. You can control what good your wealth does after your death. If you are inclined to leave something to charity, plan now. Not only will you receive tax benefits, but you will be setting an example for your family. For our property, it is until death do us part. For our legacy, it helps the needy as we love one another. Remember, that by preparing your estate plan, you are performing an act of love, an act that will last generations after you are gone.

GLOSSARY

Advance Directive or Advance Medical Directive. A legal form that allows you to choose a health care representative and provide end of life health care directives to your physician. The person selected as your health care representative is given the authority to make medical decisions for you whenever you are unable to speak for yourself.

Annual Exclusion. The amount of property, valued up to $14,000 per year in 2017 that you are permitted to give away to any other person each year without incurring any gift tax or filing a gift tax return. There is no limit on the number of people to whom you can give gifts in each year. If you are married, both the husband and the wife can give up to $14,000 per year to any person without payment of gift tax.

Applicable Exclusion or Exemption. The value of the assets a person can have at the time of his or her death without incurring an estate tax. In 2017, the federal exemption is $5.49 million. Some states have their own inheritance or estate tax. In 2017, the exemption amount in Oregon is $1.0 million.

Attorney-in-Fact. Sometimes this is referred to as an agent. This is a person who is given written authorization by one individual to transact business as the agent for the first person. This power is given in a written document called a Power of Attorney.

Beneficiary. A person who is named to receive benefits. A person can be a beneficiary of a trust, Will, life insurance policy, or investment account.

Beneficiary Designations. Beneficiary designations are forms which are used to designate how a specific asset will be passed to beneficiaries at your death. These beneficiary designations must be in writing and often are required to be on specific forms. Beneficiary designations are used with life insurance, pension plans, 401k plans, IRAs, and annuity death benefits.

Capital Gain. A profit that results from a disposition of a capital asset, such as a stock, bond, or real estate, where the amount realized on the disposition exceeds the purchase price.

Charitable Gift. A gift recognized by the Internal Revenue Service to a legal charity. The charity must meet special requirements under the Internal Revenue Code. If the requirements are met, the gift will be deductible for income and estate tax purposes.

Charitable Trust. A charitable trust is created for the benefit of a legal charity. Trusts can be created that provide an income to you during your lifetime with the remainder assets going to the charity upon your death or income can be provided to the charity during your lifetime with the remainder assets going to your beneficiaries at the time of your death.

Claw Back Rule. If you are transferring an existing life insurance policy to a trust and you die within three years of the date of the transfer the policy, the policy proceeds are pulled back into your estate for federal estate tax purposes and for Oregon tax purposes as if you had remained owner of the policy.

Community Property. A way of owning property under the law of the minority estates. Under community property law, when a married couple acquires property, each spouse is considered to own a one- half interest in the property.

Computer Fraud and Abuse Act (CFAA). An amendment to existing computer fraud law enacted by Congress in 1986. The CFAA was written to clarify and increase the scope of the previous version the law and also criminalized additional computer-related acts.

Credit Shelter Trust. A trust that is established at the time of death to hold assets that do not qualify for the marital deduction. The Credit Shelter Trust takes advantage of a person's lifetime exclusion and bypasses the surviving spouse's taxable estate and is not subject to estate taxes. The Credit Shelter Trust may be for the benefit of the surviving spouse, the decedent's children, and other beneficiaries. While all the assets are not subject to estate tax, when the assets are transferred to the beneficiaries upon the second spouse's death, the assets carry a cost basis to the beneficiaries and not a stepped-up fair market value basis.

Decoupled. The Oregon exemption amount has been $1.0 million for many years and there is no indication of change in the future. This creates a gap in the exemption amount created by the "decoupling" of the federal estate tax from the Oregon inheritance tax. The gap in 2017 is $4.49 million.

Digital Assets. Anything that is stored in a binary format and comes with the right to use, such as images, multimedia and textual content files (examples: email accounts, social media accounts, photo and video sharing accounts, music accounts, cloud storage, blogs, eBook accounts, video game accounts, online financial information).

Digital Account. Means an electronic system for creating, generating, sending, sharing, communicating, receiving, storing, displaying, or processing information that provides access to a *Digital Asset* stored on a *Digital Device*, regardless of the ownership of such *Digital Device*

Digital Device. Is an electronic device that can create, generate, send, share, communicate, receive, store, display, or process information, including, without limitation, desktops, laptops, tablets, peripherals, storage devices, mobile telephones, smart phones, cameras, electronic reading devices, and any similar digital device that currently exists or may exist as technology develops or such comparable items as technology develops.

Disclaimer. A refusal to accept an inheritance the beneficiary is entitled to receive. The disclaimer by the beneficiary currently must be made within nine months of the date of death.

Discretionary Trust. A trust where the beneficiaries do not have a fixed entitlement or interest in the trust funds. The trustee has the discretion to determine which of the beneficiaries are to receive the principal and income of the trust, and how much each beneficiary is to receive.

Durable Power of Attorney. A Power of Attorney is a legal document that authorizes someone to legally "step into your shoes." You can authorize your agent to do such things as sign checks and tax returns, enter into contracts, buy or sell real estate, deposit or withdraw funds, run a business, or anything else you would do for yourself. This Power of Attorney can be effective when the document is signed or it can "spring into effect" when you become disabled or incapacitated.

Executor. A person or institution appointed by a testator to carry out the terms of their Will. The term varies among different states and the person is often identified as an administrator or Personal Representative. This is the person who will handle Probate and is responsible for all assets of the estate, payment of taxes, payment of creditors, and distribution of assets to beneficiaries.

401(k) Plan. A feature of a qualified profit-sharing plan that allows employees to contribute a portion of their wages to individual accounts on a tax-deferred basis.

Fiduciary. A fiduciary is a person held to a higher standard of responsibility and duty in a position of trust. Fiduciaries include the Executor of a Will, the trustee of a trust, an agent under a Power of Attorney, or anyone responsible for holding or managing assets of another person.

Generation-Skipping Transfer Tax. A tax assessed on gifts in excess of the exclusion amount given to grandchildren, great-grandchildren, and others at least two generations below the individual making the gift. Some states have a generation-skipping transfer tax, and other states do not have this tax.

Gift Tax. A federal tax that taxes the value of a gift when it exceeds both the annual gift tax exclusion ($14,000 per person in 2017) and the applicable lifetime gift tax exclusion amount. There is a variance among states, with some states having a gift tax and other states not having a gift tax.

Grantor-Retained Annuity Trust. A trust that provides for lifetime transfers designed to save taxes, avoid Probate, and transfer property to your heirs upon death. This is an irrevocable lifetime trust that permits you to enjoy some use of the transferred assets, avoid Probate, and save estate taxes. Generally, these trusts can be structured so that you receive income for a period of years.

Guardian. A person who cares for and is legally responsible for someone who is unable to manage their own affairs, such as an incompetent or disabled person or a minor child whose parents have died. In Oregon a Guardian is responsible for the well fare of the ward and a Conservator is responsible for managing the money of a ward.

Health Insurance Portability and Accountability Act (HIPAA). Federal privacy rule first passed by Congress in 1996 which provides important privacy rights and protections with respect to the dissemination of your health information. HIPAA also provides the ability to transfer and continue health insurance coverage for millions of American workers and their families when they change or lose their jobs

Heir. A person who receives the property or assets of a deceased person. Property can be received by Will, trust, or intestate.

Incompetence Proceeding. A legal process in a Probate court which guarantees the allegedly incompetent person due process of law.

Irrevocable Life Insurance Trust (ILIT). An irrevocable trust used to hold a life insurance policy. The proceeds of the life insurance policy are not part of the deceased person's estate and thus, reduce estate taxes.

Irrevocable Trust. A trust that cannot be changed.

Joint Tenancy. A method of holding property in joint names. It can be for two or more people with the survivor having automatic ownership of the property after the death of the other owner. This method can be used to avoid Probate.

Limited Liability Company. A form of entity that provides for limited liability for all investors with an income flow through to the investors. A limited liability company is similar to a partnership. Limited liability companies provide options for business and estate planning. Whether it is a limited liability company or a family limited partnership, businesses must have written agreements concerning ownership, operation, management, and transfer of interest.

Limited Liability Partnership. A partnership that limits the risk that a general partnership would have. This form of business is often used to transfer business assets to children at a discounted value.

Long-term Care Insurance (LTC or LTCI). An insurance product which helps provide for the cost of long-term care beyond a predetermined period. Covers care generally not covered by other health insurance, Medicare, or Medicaid.

Marital Deduction. The unlimited amount of assets that can be transferred from one spouse to another during life or at death of the first spouse without incurring any gift or estate tax cost.

Minor Trusts. Irrevocable trusts used to transfer assets from your estate to make gifts to minors while retaining control. Income and principal may be accumulated or distributed. The trust must terminate, and all trust assets distributed to the child upon reaching age 21 unless the child voluntarily consents to allow the trust to continue. Individuals often use the annual gift tax exclusion to make gifts to a minor trust.

Non-Probate Assets. Assets that transfer automatically on death such as pay on death accounts, joint tenancy property, retirement accounts.

Pay on Death Account (POD account). A special type of financial account that transfers the account to the designated person on the first death.

Pour-over Will. A Will that transfers your assets at death to a trust. The trust must be in existence at the time of death. The Will pours over the assets to the trust through the state Probate process.

Probate. A court process by which a Will is proven valid or invalid. Probate is the legal process wherein the estate of a decedent is administered. Even if there is a Will, the estate must be Probated. During Probate the court has the assets inventoried, creditors are notified and requested to make claims.

Qualified Domestic Trust (QDOT). A trust that is used along with a QTIP trust when one spouse is a non-citizen of the United States. The QDOT trust requires that if a surviving spouse is a non-citizen, the trustee must be a citizen of the United States in order for the trust to qualify to defer estate taxes.

Qualified Sub Chapter S Trust (QSST). Businesses can be run as a sub-chapter S corporation. Upon death, an S corporation election is terminated if it is acquired by a non-qualified shareholder. If a trust qualifies as a QSST, and a timely election is filed with the Internal Revenue Service, a trust can hold stock of an S corporation without the corporation being disqualified for a limited period of time.

Qualified Terminal Interest Property Trust (QTIP). A trust that requires the surviving spouse to receive all income from the trust at least annually that upon termination transfers the trust assets to persons designated by the deceased individual. This trust qualifies for the unlimited marital deduction. Trust assets are included in the taxable estate of the second spouse to die.

Required Minimum Distributions (RMD). This is the amount that the federal government requires you to withdraw annually from your 401k plan, traditional IRAs, and employer-sponsored retirement plans.

Revocable Living Trust. A trust created while a person is alive. It can be amended, changed, terminated any time while the trustor or maker of the trust is competent. This is often referred to as an inter vivos trust. The trust becomes irrevocable upon your death.

Self-Cancelling Installment Note (SCIN). A technique used by estate planners when transferring a family business from one generation to another involves selling the business in exchange for a self-cancelling installment note ("SCIN"). A SCIN is a debt obligation which, in the event of the death of the seller/creditor, will be extinguished with the remaining note balance automatically canceled.

Spendthrift Trust. A trust created for the benefit of a person (often unable to control his spending) that gives an independent trustee full authority to make decisions as to how the trust funds may be spent for the benefit of the beneficiary.

Spousal Share. Some states have statutes that require that for married couples, a minimum percentage of the assets of the first spouse to die are transferred to the surviving spouse.

State Estate or Inheritance Tax. Many states have decoupled from the federal estate tax system and individuals in those states are subject to both Federal and State estate or inheritance tax. The treatment of taxes varies from state to state because of federal tax credits and the different state laws. For example, in Oregon, there is a $1.0 million exemption for state inheritance taxes, but there is no gift tax.

Stretch-Out. The IRS has provided an option that will allow a stretch out of inherited qualified plans or IRAs to allow the plan assets to accumulate tax deferred and avoid immediate income and estate taxes. A benefit of qualified plans and IRAs are tax deferrals which maximize the growth of assets within the plan.

Tax or Cost Basis. This is a term used for tax purposes that is used to compute the taxable gain for income tax purposes on the sale of property. Assets that are in the estate of the deceased person at the time of death take the fair market value of the assets at the date of death or six months after the date of death, whichever evaluation date is elected. This means that the appreciation of assets in an estate is not subject to federal income tax if passed to the beneficiary at the time of death. On the other hand, assets in a credit shelter trust are not subject to estate tax at the death of the second spouse, by they do not get the advantage of the step-up in basis to the fair market value.

Testamentary Trust. A trust that becomes effective upon death.

Trust. An agreement when one person holds property for the benefit of another. The person creating the trust is the trustor, grantor, or settler, depending on the particular state. The person with a fiduciary duty holding the property is called a trustee. The person or persons for whose benefit the property is held is called the beneficiary. The trustee holds legal title to the property, and the beneficiary holds equitable title to the property. The document establishing the trust is called the trust agreement. A trust can be effective during the trustor's life (inter vivos trust) or become effective upon the trustor's death (testamentary trust). If a trust can be revoked or modified, it is a revocable trust. If a trust cannot be revoked or modified, it is an irrevocable trust.

Trustee. The fiduciary who holds legal title to trust property and who is responsible for managing the trust assets.

Uniform Gift to Minors Act. A method of transferring assets to minors during your lifetime, which requires mandatory distribution to minors at a certain age.

Uniform Trust Code (UTC). A law in the United States, which, although not binding, is influential in the states, and used by many as a model for their law. A majority of states have adopted some substantive form of the UTC.

Will. A legal document that transfers property at a person's death to those individuals he or she has designated. Sometimes referred to as a **Last Will and Testament** this document only affects property owned at the time of death. Usually, a person will appoint an Executor to manage his estate in the Will. If there is a conflict between a beneficiary form and a distribution of property in the Will, the beneficiary form designation will prevail.

Made in the USA
Columbia, SC
09 September 2017